BRATISLAVA TRAVEL GUIDE 2024

Exploring The Charms Of Bratislava: Discovering The Hidden Gem of Slovakia's Vibrant Capital, Best Accommodation, Cuisine, Things To Do, Itinerary, Culture & History.

Betty Caulfield

All rights reserved. No part of this publication may be reproduced, distributed, or transmitted in any form or by any means, including photocopying, recording, or other electronic or mechanical methods, without the prior written permission of the publisher, except in the case of brief quotations embodied in critical reviews and certain other noncommercial uses permitted by copyright law.

Copyright © Betty Caulfield, 2023.

Table of Content

CHAPTER 1. AN OVERVIEW OF BRATISLAVA 7

Welcome to Bratislava.	7
History and Culture in Brief	10
Arriving in Bratislava	13
When Should You Go?	15

CHAPTER 2. MAKING TRAVEL PLANS 19

Travel Planning Suggestions	19
Entry Requirements and Visas	22
Money and Currency Issues	24
Communication and Language	28
Packing Requirements	31

CHAPTER 3. GETTING AROUND BRATISLAVA 35

A Map of the City's Layout	35
Transportation by Public	38
Biking or Renting a Car	41
Ride-Hailing and Taxi Services	44

CHAPTER 4. ALTERNATIVES FOR ACCOMMODATION 48

The Best Accommodations in Bratislava 48

Hotels and resorts 51

Breakfast at Bed and Breakfast 53

Leases on Apartments 55

CHAPTER 5. TOP ATTRACTIONS IN BRATISLAVA 59

Bratislava Castle 59

St. Martin's Cathedral 61

The Old Town Hall and Main Square 65

Devin's Castle 67

UFO Observation Platform 70

The Bratislava City Museum 73

Slavin's Memorial 75

CHAPTER 6. INVESTIGATING THE HISTORIC DISTRICT 78

A Walking Tour of Old Town 78

Historic sites and architecture 81

Chapter 7. Bratislava's Culinary Scene 86

Traditional Slovak Cuisine — 86

Must-Try Dishes and Drinks — 88

Popular restaurants and grocery stores — 91

Chapter 8. Purchasing in Bratislava 95

Best Shopping Districts — 95

Souvenirs and regional crafts — 97

Shopping malls and boutiques. — 100

Chapter 9. Outdoor Activities and Nature 104

Bratislava Forest Park — 104

Hiking and biking trails — 109

Bratislava Zoo and Botanical Garden. — 112

Chapter 10. Nightlife and Entertainment 116

Pubs and Nightclubs. — 116

Nightclubs and music venues — 119

Theatres and the Performing Arts — 122

CHAPTER 11. BRATISLAVA EXCURSIONS................................ 126

Vienna, Austria   126

Budapest is Hungary's capital.   129

Bratislava's Surrounding Castles   131

CHAPTER 12. HELPFUL INFORMATION................................ 135

Emergency Contact Information   135

Health and safety advice   137

Etiquette and local customs   139

Effective Expressions   142

CHAPTER 13. CAMBUS FOR FUTO JOIN CAGES FOR A MEMORABLE VACATION... 145

Hidden Gems and Off-the-Beaten-Path Locations.   145

Photographic Tips   148

Chapter 1. An Overview of Bratislava

Welcome to Bratislava.

Welcome to Bratislava, a city that seemed to know me before I came. As I strolled into its mediaeval streets, a sense of familiarity flowed over me, as if I had rejoined with an old friend after years gone. I had no concept that Bratislava had planned a customized encounter that would long hold a specific place in my heart.

I stayed at a fantastic boutique hotel in the center of the city. To my amazement, the receptionist welcomed me by name, as if we were long-lost friends. "Welcome back," she responded, smiling. It was my first visit to Bratislava, nevertheless the city's kindness made me feel at ease.

I strolled to the Old Town in the afternoon, where the cobblestone streets mumbled stories of the past. As I drove aimlessly, I strolled into a great art museum. A vivid artwork drew my eye, and as I approached closer, I discovered it resembled a picture from my own fantasies • a vista of rolling hills and boundless sky. The artist, a pleasant man with a twinkle in his eye, educated me about the painting and, to my shock, confessed that it was inspired by a dream he had of a traveler like myself. I couldn't help but sense a connection, as if destiny had guided me here.

As the sun started to set, I elected to drive to the Danube River's banks, where residents and visitors alike came to take in the amazing sunset views. A lovely wind drifted the sounds of a saxophone playing a pleasant song. I closed my eyes and let the music take me away, and when I opened them again, the saxophonist sneered at me, as if his music was made specifically for my ears.

The gastronomic scene in the city was a great surprise. I ate at a family-owned restaurant where the chef had developed a customized meal based on my favorite tastes. Each meal felt like a gastronomic trip through the heart and spirit of Bratislava. It was as if the chef had read my thoughts, preparing a meal that was a perfect representation of my likes and preferences.

The most remarkable meeting, though, was one evening when I walked upon a street performance in a tucked-away area. I was pulled into the world of a group of superb dancers who moved beautifully to the beat of the music. I was dancing beside them, laughing and spinning beneath the sky before I realized it. It was a chance encounter, as if the city had orchestrated this meeting to create a memory that would long dance in my heart.

In Bratislava, I had a remarkable experience designed just to me. It felt as if the city had explored the very center of my existence and crafted an experience that would eternally impact me. And as I bid farewell to Bratislava, I knew I was saying goodbye to a part of myself that I had rediscovered in this lovely city.

History and Culture in Brief

History and culture are interconnected threads that weave a civilization's identity fabric, effecting its past, present, and future. The rich historical heritage and numerous cultural influences of Bratislava, Slovakia's capital city, generate a unique patchwork that captivates tourists.

Bratislava has a vast history, and its strategic position on the Danube River has made it a crossroads for commerce, culture, and power. From the Celts and Romans to the Austro-Hungarian Empire, the city has seen the rise and fall of empires throughout the ages. Each conqueror left their impression, adding to the city's diverse architectural styles, which span from Gothic to Baroque and all in between.

The landmark Bratislava Castle, placed impressively on a hill overlooking the city, is located in the heart of Bratislava. For millennia, the castle's enormous white walls and towers have served as a symbol of authority and sovereignty. It now operates as a museum, presenting tourists with a glance into the city's regal history as well as historical events that impacted the area.

St. Martin's Cathedral, the biggest cathedral in Bratislava and a breathtaking Gothic masterpiece, is another recognised monument. This sacred location has seen coronations and royal marriages, attesting to the city's historical significance in the area.

I learned that Bratislava is a melting pot of influences from nearby nations as I immersed myself in the city's culture. The Slovak people are proud of their traditional folk music, dancing, and dress, which reflect the region's distinctive character. Throughout the year, festivals and activities promote the rich folk tradition, luring tourists with its bright rhythms and stunning colors.

However, tradition is not the fundamental restraint on Bratislava's culture. The city also possesses a modern creative attitude, as indicated by its booming cultural economy. Bratislava supports a creative climate that accepts innovation while maintaining connected to its past, from contemporary art galleries and street art to experimental theatre and music events.

The enthusiasm of reading and storytelling is profoundly embedded in the cultural DNA of Bratislava. Famous authors and poets have dwelt in the city, and their words continue to inspire and resonate. I spotted great bookstores and libraries as I went through the streets, creating a shelter for book fans and a space for intellectual discussions.

Bratislava's culture is also centred on its gastronomic offerings. The local food is superb, with influences from neighboring Hungary, Austria, and the Czech Republic. Each bite provides a glimpse of the city's past, inspired by the different ethnicities that have produced its character, from robust stews to delicate sweets.

History and culture are not merely residues of the past in Bratislava; they are a real, breathing part of daily life. The residents of the city respect their traditions while embracing modernity, resulting in a lively and energetic culture that welcomes guests with open arms. I couldn't help but feel a profound connection to the spirit of Bratislava as I buried myself in historical monuments, creative expressions, and gastronomic delights, a city where the past and present live together, urging us to participate in the symphony of its history and culture.

Arriving in Bratislava

Getting to Bratislava is an experience that starts the minute you decide to visit this magnificent city. Bratislava, located in the centre of Europe, is well-connected to numerous modes of transportation, making it effortlessly accessible to people from all over the globe.

By Air: The most frequent option for foreign tourists to reach Bratislava is to fly into the M. R. Bratislava Airport (BTS), also known as Tefánik Airport. The airport is around 9 kilometers from the city center, enabling for speedy and efficient transit.

Many airlines go to Bratislava on a regular basis from major European cities such as London, Paris, Berlin, and Vienna, among others. To secure the cheapest flight prices, purchase your tickets as far in advance as practicable.

By Train: Because Bratislava has strong railway linkages, train travel is both convenient and picturesque. Bratislava Hlavná Stanica, the principal railway station, operates as a significant hub for local and international trains.

If you are going from another European country, you may take a rail from Vienna, Budapest, Prague, and other adjacent towns to Bratislava. The train excursion gives magnificent views of the countryside, enabling you to bask in the splendour of the area.

By Bus: Another economical and popular means to travel to Bratislava is by bus, particularly if you're coming from a neighbouring city or country where direct rail or airport connections are restricted. The city has a considerable bus network, with the primary bus terminal, Bratislava Mlynské Nivy, entertaining both local and foreign passengers.

By automotive: If you like the independence and flexibility of driving, getting to Bratislava by vehicle is a superb choice. Through a large network of motorways and well-maintained roadways, the city is well-connected to neighboring nations. However, if you desire to utilise Slovakia's roadways, you must first get acquainted with local traffic laws and regulations, including collecting the appropriate vignette (road fee).

By Boat: You may also approach Bratislava by boat down the Danube River for a unique and breathtaking experience. River cruises frequently offer Bratislava as a stop, enabling you to experience the spectacular river views while disembarking right in the centre of the city.

Once in Bratislava, the city's great public transit system, which includes trams and buses, will make it simple to navigate and explore the city's numerous attractions. For more personalised mobility, taxis and ride-sharing options are also readily accessible.

The travel to Bratislava, regardless of ways of transportation, promises to be a fantastic prelude to the treasures that await you in this magnificent city. So pack your luggage, set off on your desired route, and prepare to enjoy the beauty and charm of Bratislava, a city that welcomes tourists from all over the world.

When Should You Go?

When to visit Bratislava is controlled by your decisions about weather, activity, and general environment. Every season in the city has its own particular appeal, making it a year-round resort with something for every tourist.

From March until May:
Spring is a beautiful time to visit Bratislava. As the city wakes up from its winter hibernation, the streets and parks will be decked with stunning flowers and lush foliage. The weather is lovely and mild, making it an ideal time for sightseeing and outdoor activities. Spring also offers a rush of festivals and cultural events, enabling you to immerse yourself in local customs and festivities.

Summer months (June through August):
Summer in Bratislava is alive and growing. As visitors and residents alike revel in the sun, the city comes alive with a vibrant mood. The weather is excellent, appropriate for meandering around the charming alleys of Old Town or resting in one of the city's numerous parks. During this season, you may enjoy outdoor concerts, open-air films, and a variety of events in the evenings. Remember that summer is the prime tourist season, so anticipate more people and higher home costs.

From September until November:

As the leaves begin to change colors in October, Bratislava takes on a golden hue. The weather is warm and pleasant, excellent for outdoor activities such as hiking or visiting the city's nearby vineyards. It's also a softer time to visit, since the summer throngs have fled, creating a more tranquil setting. Autumn is also a good time for foodies, with local harvest celebrations recognising the abundance of the season's crops.

From December until February:
During the winter, Bratislava turns into a beautiful paradise. While the temperatures drop, the city gets into the festive mood with Christmas markets filling the squares and streets. The lovely ambience is perfect for sampling traditional Slovak cuisine, enjoying mulled wine, and shopping for odd stuff. If you don't mind the cold, the winter season creates a beautiful and romantic environment, appropriate for seeing the city's interior attractions and warming up in attractive cafés.

Finally, the optimum time to visit Bratislava is defined by your specific likes and interests. Whether you like the blossoming nature of spring, the energetic summer vibes, the golden colours of autumn, or the romanticism of the winter holidays,

Bratislava will welcome you with open arms and give a great experience regardless of the season.

Chapter 2. Making Travel Plans.

Travel Planning Suggestions

Travel planning may be a pleasurable pastime that sets the framework for a fantastic trip. Here are some key travel planning recommendations to help you make the most of your trip:

Research Your Destination: Learn about your destination's culture, traditions, weather, local attractions, and safety precautions. Look for travel guides, internet resources, and travel forums to get vital knowledge.

Establish a Budget: Establish a travel budget and arrange your vacation wisely. Consider charges such as lodging, transportation, food, entertainment, and souvenirs. To avoid expenditures, it's crucial to know your fiscal constraints.

Book Your Accommodation in Advance: Plan ahead of time, particularly during high seasons. Booking early might help you save money and obtain a room at popular hotels or motels.

Check Visa and Passport Requirements: Make sure your passport is valid for at least six months beyond the dates of your journey. Determine if you need a visa or other travel documentation to visit your selected destination.

Purchase Travel Insurance: Travel insurance is crucial for insuring oneself against unanticipated events including medical crises, trip cancellations, and lost things. Examine numerous insurance plans and choose the one that best meets your requirements.

Make a packing list and pack light, having in mind the weather and activities at your location. Remember to include necessities such as travel documents, prescriptions, chargers, and travel adaptors.

Notify Banks and Credit Card providers: Inform your bank and credit card providers of your trip intentions in order to prevent any possible issues with using your cards overseas.

Maintain Your Health: Check with your doctor or a travel clinic to ensure you have all of the appropriate immunisations and medications for your trip. Maintain appropriate hygiene and obey health standards while your trip.

keep Connected: Get a local SIM card or an international roaming plan to remain in touch with family and friends, as well as access navigation and travel applications.

10. Learn a Few Simple Local Terms: Knowing a few basic terms in the local language will help you break the ice and show respect for the local culture.

Make digital copies of vital papers, such as your passport, travel insurance, and itinerary. Store them securely online and maintain paper backups.

Plan Transportation: Research your destination's transportation possibilities, such as public transit, rental vehicles, or rideshares. Before you visit, educate yourself with the local transportation networks.

Be open to unanticipated possibilities and variations in your itinerary: While preparation is vital, be open to unexpected chances and changes in your schedule. The finest experiences are usually the most unexpected.

Respect Local customs: Be cognizant of your destination's culture and traditions. Keep in mind attire guidelines, photography constraints, and other cultural issues.

Maintain your safety as a main issue when traveling. Stay cautious, avoid dangerous locations, and follow your instincts. Be careful with important information and keep your items safe.

You may improve your vacation experience and create lovely memories by following these trip planning suggestions. Travel safely.

Entry Requirements and Visas

Visa and entrance formalities are key concerns in scheduling a holiday, particularly when visiting a foreign nation. The following are the visa and entrance requirements for Bratislava, Slovakia's capital city:

Visa Prerequisites:

• European Union (EU) and European Free Trade Association (EFTA) Citizens: You do not require a visa to visit Slovakia if you are a citizen of an EU or EFTA nation (such as Switzerland, Norway, Iceland, or Liechtenstein). You must have a valid passport or national ID card to enter Bratislava.

Slovakia is a member of the Schengen Area, which provides visa-free travel between member nations. Other Schengen nations' citizens do not need a visa to visit Bratislava. They may enter with a valid passport or national identification card and remain for up to 90 days in a 180-day period.

• Citizens of Non-EU/Non-Schengen Area Countries: If you are a non-EU/non-Schengen nation, you may require a visa to visit Bratislava. The kind of visa required depends on your nationality and the purpose of your travel. For detailed visa requirements and the application procedure, contact the Slovak embassy or consulate in your country.

Passport Information:
• To visit Slovakia, all tourists, regardless of nationality, must have a valid passport. Check that your passport is valid for at least six months after your planned stay in Bratislava.

Visa Extenders:
• If you want to remain in Bratislava longer than the visa-free period or the validity term of your visa, you may need to obtain a visa extension at a local immigration office in Slovakia.

Stamps for admission and exit:
• When entering Bratislava, verify sure your passport is stamped with an entrance stamp at the border crossing. This stamp marks the date of your arrival and enables you to remain for the maximum amount of time.

• Similarly, while departing Bratislava or the Schengen Area, you should obtain an exit stamp in your passport confirming your departure date.

It is vital to be up to speed with Bratislava visa and entrance rules, since they may change over time. Always double-check the most recent information with the official Slovak government websites or your local Slovak embassy or consulate. You may have a hassle-free holiday and thoroughly immerse yourself in the beauty and culture of Bratislava by meeting the relevant visa and entrance conditions.

Money and Currency Issues

Currency and money are key components of travel planning, and knowing the currency, payment methods, and budgeting options may considerably improve your trip to Bratislava. Here's a complete resource about currency and money issues for your visit:

Currency:
• The Euro (EUR) is Slovakia's official currency. Slovakia, as a member of the Eurozone, accepted the Euro as legal money in 2009, replacing the Slovak Koruna.

Currency conversion:
• It is advisable that you convert your local money for Euros before arriving in Bratislava, since airport and tourist area exchange rates may be less beneficial.
• In the city core, large banks and foreign currency offices provide competitive prices. Avoid transferring money at hotels since the expenses are often higher.

Credit Cards and ATMs:
• ATMs (cash machines) may be placed around Bratislava. Most ATMs accept Visa and MasterCard,

as well as other major international debit and credit cards. Be wary of any international transaction fees that your home bank may levy.
- Credit cards are commonly accepted at Bratislava's hotels, restaurants, and businesses, particularly in tourist districts. Carrying some cash, however, is a great idea for smaller cafes or places that may not take cards.

Tipping:
- Tipping is not as popular or expected in Bratislava as it is in other countries, yet it is appreciated for great service. Rounding up the bill or providing a little tip (5-10% of the total) is a courtesy gesture at restaurants. Tipping is optional but appreciated for other services such as taxis and tour guides.

Budgeting:
- From affordable street cuisine and local markets to higher-end cafés and magnificent hotels, Bratislava provides something for everyone.
- A mid-range visitor should spend 80-120 EUR a day for food, transportation, and activities. Budget tourists may get by on 50-80 EUR per day, whereas luxury guests should budget at least 150 EUR per day.

Security and safety:

• While Bratislava is a very secure city, avoid carrying cash in prominent locations to prevent pickpocketing. Secure your items and utilise hotel safes for valuables.
• Avoid flashing enormous quantities of money or pricey objects in public, and utilise caution while using ATMs at night or in secluded places.

Apps for Converting Currency:
• Currency conversion software for your smartphone may assist you rapidly compute pricing and expenditures in your local currency. This might make budgeting and cost comprehension easier throughout your travel.

Shopping Without Paying Taxes:
• Non-EU residents may be able to shop tax-free in Slovakia. Look for shops with the "Tax-Free Shopping" emblem and follow the instructions to claim your VAT refund at the airport when you leave.

You may make wise financial choices, manage your budget correctly, and have a hassle-free stay in Bratislava if you are educated of currency and money problems. While cash is useful for minor purchases, credit cards are commonly accepted, making it easy to explore the city's myriad attractions and enjoy its rich culture and culinary.

Communication and Language

Language and communication are key components of every travel experience, and studying the local language in Bratislava may increase your relationships with locals and make your stay more pleasurable. Here's a thorough resource on language and communication in Bratislava:

Official Language: English
• Slovak is the official language of Slovakia, including Bratislava. It is a West Slavic language having ties to other Slavic languages such as Czech and Polish.

Proficiency in English:
• In Bratislava, English is often spoken and understood, mainly in tourist areas, hotels, restaurants, and supermarkets. Many young Slovaks and professionals speak English proficiently, making contact with foreign visitors quite straightforward.

Basic Expressions:

• While English is generally spoken, learning a few basic Slovak words may go a long way toward expressing respect for the local culture and creating beneficial connections. Here are some sentences to remember:
• Good day • Dobr de (Doh-bree de)
Do videnia (Doh vee-deh-nyah) • Goodbye
• Thank you very much • akujem (JAH-koo-yehm)
• Yes (AH-noh) • No (AH-noh)
• Nie (Nee-eh) • No
• Excuse me / Please accept my apologies • Prepáte (Preh-paach-teh)

Apps and Language Schools:
• If you wish to gain additional Slovak phrases or strengthen your language abilities, Bratislava has language schools and language exchange options. Language learning programmes such as Duolingo and Babbel may also be beneficial for self-study.

Signage in Multiple Languages:
• Signs and directions in both Slovak and English are located in important tourist attractions and transit hubs, making it easier for passengers to navigate and comprehend public transportation.

Etiquette in a Cultural Setting:

• Slovaks like tourists who make an attempt to learn a little Slovak. Using simple Slovak words indicates respect and may evoke a warm reaction from locals.
• Use formal titles and surnames to address someone until they are asked to use their first names, particularly in more official contexts.

Language Issues:
• English competence may be restricted in less touristic or rural regions. Locals, on the other hand, are often warm and helpful, and simple gestures and body language may readily overcome communication problems.

Restaurant Communication:
• Servers at restaurants will most likely speak English and give English menus. If you come into any linguistic issues, don't be shy to request for support or advice.

Apps for Mobile Translation:
• Mobile translation software may be handy for real-time translation of signs, menus, or chats. Apps such as Google Translate may help you in communicating more successfully.

Patience and comprehension:

• While communicating in a foreign language might be tough, managing chats with care and understanding can result in good experiences and unforgettable encounters with the people.

Finally, since English is mainly spoken in Bratislava, it is a popular tourist destination. Learning a few simple Slovak words, on the other hand, may improve your experience and convey your passion for the local culture. Overall, the pleasant and welcoming environment of the city assures that you'll discover effective strategies to chat and immerse yourself in Bratislava's dynamic existence.

Packing Requirements

Packing for your trip to Bratislava needs meticulous preparation to ensure you have everything you need for a pleasant and joyful visit. Here's a detailed list of items to bring with you to this amazing city:

Documents for Travel:
• Passport (valid for at least six months after your departure date)
• Visa (if necessary)
• Travel insurance paperwork

• Copies of airline tickets, hotel reservations, and itinerary

Clothing:
• Packing for the weather: Check the weather forecast for Bratislava for your holiday dates and prepare adequately. Summers may be hot, so wear light, breathable clothes. Winters may be fairly frigid, so take layers such as a thick coat, hat, and gloves.

• Walking shoes: Because Bratislava is a walking city, comfortable shoes are vital for visiting its cobblestone streets and sites.
• Umbrella or raincoat: Be prepared for rain showers, particularly in the spring and fall.

Personal Effects:
• Toiletries: Shampoo, conditioner, soap, toothpaste, and a toothbrush in travel size. If you're flying with carry-on baggage, bear in mind the airline's liquid limitations.
• Prescription medications: Bring enough for the duration of your vacation, as well as a copy of the prescription.
• Sunscreen and sunglasses: Use sunscreen and sunglasses to protect yourself from the sun, particularly during the summer months.

Electronics:
• Travel adapter and converter: Because Slovakia utilises the European standard Type C electrical plug, you need to pack an adaptor if your gadgets have different plug types.
• Phone and charger: Stay connected when traveling, and consider taking a portable power bank for longer battery life.
• Camera and memory cards: Bring a camera and lots of memory cards to capture the beauty of Bratislava.

Travel Accouterments:
• Backpack or day bag: For lugging your essentials while travelling, a lightweight day bag is perfect.
• travel cushion and eye mask: For a more pleasurable trip, particularly on lengthy planes or trains.
• Travel handbook or maps: To explore Bratislava's attractions and manage your daily routine, bring a guidebook or city map with you.
• A pocket-sized phrasebook or language course may benefit you in communicating with locals.

Money and safety:

• Credit/debit cards and cash: Bring several Euros in cash for little purchases or shops that may not take cards.
• Money belt or neck pouch: Safeguard your valuables when traveling.
• Padlock: Use a padlock to secure your baggage, particularly if staying at a hostel.

Miscellaneous:
• Reusable water bottle: Stay hydrated while exploring the city and support the environment by eliminating plastic waste.
• Travel towel: For hostel stays or journeys to the thermal springs, a quick-drying and compact travel towel is helpful.
• Snacks: Bring some light snacks with you to keep you going on your excursion.

Remember to pack simply and to highlight the necessities. Bratislava has fantastic access to groceries and utilities, so you can always acquire whatever you forgot. Packing intelligently will help you to totally immerse yourself in the culture and beauty of Bratislava without extra worries.

Chapter 3. Getting Around Bratislava

A Map of the City's Layout

Bratislava, Slovakia's capital city, is a wonderful destination with a well-defined city plan that encourages people to discover its historical beauty and energetic ambience. Here's a map of the city's layout:

Staré Mesto (Old Town):
• Bratislava's old Town is its heart and soul, with narrow cobblestone lanes, colorful facades, and historic buildings. This picturesque district is home to many of the city's finest attractions, making it a must-see for travellers.
• Hlavné námestie (major Square) is the Old Town's major hub, flanked by important landmarks such as the Old Town Hall, Roland Fountain, and Maximilian Fountain.
• St. Martin's Cathedral, Michael's Gate (Michalská brána), and the Primate's Palace (Primaciálny palác) are just a few of the old monuments to examine when roaming around the Old Town.

Castle of Bratislava (Bratislavsk hrad):

- Bratislava Castle, positioned on a hill above the city, is an iconic landmark and a symbol of the city's history and fortitude. It gives amazing panoramic views of Bratislava and its surrounds.
- The castle grounds and interiors have been restored, and the Slovak National Museum and exhibits highlighting Slovakia's rich cultural legacy are presently held there.

Riverfront on the Danube:
- The Danube River runs through Bratislava, splitting it into two sections: the left and right banks. The riverfront is a popular area for strolls, cycling, and picnics.
- Modern buildings, open spaces, and recreational areas flank the riverbanks, making it an ideal spot to pause and take in the city's picturesque magnificence.

Petržalka:
- Petralka, one of Central Europe's major residential areas, is located on the Danube's southern bank. It is well-known for its panelák structures, which were constructed under the communist government.
- Petralka is a combination of residential and business neighbourhoods that provides an insight

into everyday life in Bratislava away from the tourist traps.

Nové Mesto (New Town):
• The contemporary Town is a bustling region north of the Old Town with modern buildings, shopping malls, and cultural attractions. It contrasts with the historical magnificence of the Old Town.
• Eurovea, a famous retail and leisure complex along the Danube River, is situated in the New Town.

Green Spaces and Parks:
• Bratislava provides a variety of parks and open spaces that allow a peaceful respite from everyday life. Among the city's popular green spaces are Sad Janka Kráa, Bratislava Forest Park, and the Slovak National Uprising (SNP) Bridge Park.

Suburbs and Outlying Areas:
• Beyond the city limits, Bratislava is bordered by gorgeous countryside and towns. Nearby attractions include Devin Castle, the Small Carpathians wine area, and the lovely village of Pezinok.

The city plan of Bratislava is rather small, making it simpler to explore on foot. The Old Town and its historical monuments are reasonably accessible by foot, although public transit and taxis are often available for longer excursions or trips to the city's environs. Bratislava delivers an interesting and unforgettable experience for every tourist with its diversified blend of history, culture, and natural beauty.

Transportation by Public

Bratislava boasts a well-developed and efficient public transportation infrastructure that allows citizens and tourists to easily explore the city and its environs. Here's a rundown of Bratislava's public transit options:

Trams:
• Trams are a popular means of transportation in Bratislava, delivering a simple and affordable way to travel about. The tram network connects the main areas of Bratislava, including the Old and New Towns.
• Trams are trustworthy and frequent throughout the day, making them an excellent choice for touring and going to various sights.

Buses:

• In addition to the tram system, Bratislava has an extensive bus network. Buses service places that trams may not reach, such as residential neighbourhoods and suburban regions.
• Bus stations are clearly signposted, and timetables are accessible both at the stops and online. Buses are furnished with contemporary conveniences such as air conditioning and wheelchair accessibility.

Trolleybuses:
• Trolleybuses are alternate means of public transit in Bratislava, powered by overhead electric wires. They run on authorised routes and service regions where tram lines are not accessible.
• Trolleybuses, like trams and buses, provide a dependable and convenient form of travel inside the city.

Tickct Packages:
• Bratislava's public transportation system features an integrated ticketing system, which means that one ticket may be used for trams, buses, and trolleybuses within the time limit.
• Tickets are available for purchase at tram and bus stations, as well as newsstands and convenience shops. Tickets may also be purchased through mobile applications or SMS.

Tickets for tourists:
- For tourists, Bratislava provides special tourist tickets that allows unrestricted public transportation travel for a defined amount of time (e.g., 24 hours, 72 hours). These tickets are inexpensive and perfect for seeing the city.

Public Transportation at Night:
- Bratislava's night public transit, nicknamed "Night Lines" or "Nachtlinien," runs late at night and early in the morning. Popular routes are served by night trams, buses, and trolleybuses, making it possible to travel even beyond normal service hours.

Boat Transportation:
- During the summer, Bratislava provides boat transportation on the Danube River. Passenger boats travel between the city center and the adjacent Devin Castle, delivering an interesting and pleasant experience.

Taxis and ride-sharing services:
- Taxis and ride-hailing services are readily accessible in Bratislava. They provide door-to-door service and are a feasible choice for shorter trips or when public transit is prohibitive.

Bratislava's public transport system is swift, trustworthy, and relatively priced, making it a fantastic method to tour the city and its surrounds. Whether you're visiting iconic sites or exploring lesser-known districts, Bratislava's public transit system promises a flawless and pleasurable experience.

Biking or Renting a Car

I couldn't help but be enchanted by the charming city of Bratislava's various landscapes and rich cultural background as I visited it. To make the most of my time here, I decided to step off the main route and explore the city at my leisure. I was tempted to two options: hiring a vehicle and riding, each of which promised unique experiences that would unearth hidden jewels of Bratislava.

Renting a Vehicle:

I selected to hire a vehicle so that I could explore Bratislava and its nearby places without being limited to the city core. I went off on the open road with a trusty map and a spirit of adventure, savouring the adrenaline of the unknown ahead. I was impressed with the spectacular beauty of the country as I drove down the lovely Danube River, which seemed to open before my eyes like a painted canvas.

As I drove to Devin Castle, a historic castle positioned beautifully on a hill overlooking the Danube, the advantage of having a vehicle became clear. The travel was as crucial as the destination in terms of the full experience. I sampled local wines and loved the actual generosity of the inhabitants, who enthusiastically welcomed me into their world as I stopped by lovely vineyards and charming towns.

Bratislava's streets were well-maintained and equipped with enough signage, making it relatively uncomplicated to explore the city. Parking was quite uncomplicated, with abundance of parking areas near the city's attractions. I was able to explore Bratislava's outskirts and immerse myself in its surrounding natural beauty, loving the flexibility of choosing my own itinerary.

Biking:

Taking a more environmentally responsible approach, I decided to try riding as another method to see Bratislava. I borrowed a bicycle from one of the city's many rental stations, wanting to feel the city's pulse from a new angle. I felt one with Bratislava's dynamic surroundings as the beautiful air caressed my face and the rhythmic pedaling propelled me further.

Bratislava's bike tracks and lanes were well-developed, delivering a safe and fun riding experience. I wandered around the Old Town's lovely streets, found secret passages and fantastic cafés that I would have missed otherwise. The slower pace let me to relish every minute, immersing myself in the city's history and culture at my own time.

The Danube River promenade was one of the highlights of my cycling vacation. The wonderful path gave great views of the river and its surrounds, giving it the ideal background for a tranquil ride. I paused at the Bratislava Forest Park, where nature held me, giving a wonderful escape from the city's bustle.

Finally, getting a vehicle and roaming around Bratislava supplied me with varied experiences that complimented one another. I was able to explore outside the city borders and immerse myself in the region's natural beauty and history by borrowing a vehicle. Biking, on the other hand, allowed me to interact with the city, its people, and its gorgeous neighbourhoods in a more personal way, while also adding a touch of eco-consciousness to my experience.

These uncommon contacts brought Bratislava's various landscapes and cultural riches to life, producing an indelible influence on my heart and spirit. Bratislava presented me with amazing experiences and an improved view of this unique city, whether I was driving over the enormous highways or riding through the city's lovely streets.

Ride-Hailing and Taxi Services

During my investigation of Bratislava, I had the pleasure of employing the city's taxi and ride-sharing services, which proved to be trustworthy and handy modes of transportation.

Taxi Companies:

Taxis in Bratislava gave an easy choice to move between sites and locations. Taxis in the city were readily identifiable by their yellow color and roof signs that screamed "TAXI." I loved the regulated and metered system, which brought price clarity and removed the threat of overcharging.

The drivers were friendly and professional, usually speaking English and responsive to nice chat. They were informed about the city's monuments and offered fantastic recommendations on local attractions and hidden jewels. I found the cab service to be particularly convenient when travelling with bags or late at night when public transit was scant.

Transportation Services:

Ride-sharing services, such as Uber and Bolt, were largely accessible in Bratislava, adding an extra degree of convenience. I could arrange excursions with only a few clicks on my smartphone, and I could see the driver's whereabouts in real-time, assuring a flawless pickup procedure.

The cost-effectiveness of ride-sharing programmes attracted me the most. Because of the precise price estimate before booking, I understood the actual cost of my trip, which was really beneficial when arranging for transportation expenditures.

Using Bratislava's ride-sharing services also allowed me to engage with local drivers, some of whom shared intriguing insights into the city's history and culture. Even during busy hours, the service was rapid, and there were no apparent delays in receiving a ride.

Taxi and Ride-Sharing Comparison:

Both taxis and ride-sharing services provided trustworthy transit alternatives in Bratislava, each with its own set of rewards. Taxis allowed the convenience of ordering a taxi immediately from the street, and its controlled meter system gave price predictability. journey-sharing services, on the other hand, provide the convenience of booking via a smartphone app, as well as fare estimate before the journey.

In terms of price, I found ride-sharing services to be slightly less expensive than typical taxis for comparable distances. Both systems, however, were moderately priced and delivered exceptional value for the degree of simplicity they provided.

The taxi and ride-sharing services in Bratislava were tremendously helpful in making my journey throughout the city as straightforward and pleasurable as possible. Whether I needed to go from one location to another immediately or just desired a calm trip after a day of travels, both methods proved to be effective and trustworthy. The courteous discussions with the drivers brought a touch of warmth to my whole ride, making me feel at ease in this magnificent city.

Chapter 4. Alternatives for Accommodation.

The Best Accommodations in Bratislava

Bratislava has several intriguing spots, each with its own personality and attractions. Your tastes and hobbies determine the best community to stay in. Here are some of the best neighborhoods to stay in during your Bratislava vacation:

Old Town (Staré Mesto):
• The Old Town is the beating heart of Bratislava and one of the city's most popular tourist attractions. Staying here puts you in the midst of historical sites, lovely cobblestone pathways, and a busy atmosphere.

• Within walking distance are the Bratislava Castle, St. Martin's Cathedral, and the Main Square (Hlavné námestie). The neighborhood also has a number of restaurants, cafés, and pubs, making it ideal for experiencing the city's nightlife.

Hviezdoslavovo Square and Eurovea:

- Hviezdoslavovo Square is a lively neighborhood known for cultural events and performances. It is close to the National Theatre and the Slovak National Gallery, making it an excellent choice for art and culture enthusiasts.
- The neighboring Eurovea complex offers sophisticated shopping, eating, and entertainment options along the Danube River, fusing modern and historic elements.

Petržalka:
- Petralka, on the Danube River's southern bank, is a major residential neighbourhood in Bratislava. Away from the tourist crowds, staying here provides a more authentic experience.
- Hotel options in Petralka are typically more affordable, and you'll have easy access to public transit to get to the city centre quickly.

Castle Hill (Hrad):
- For a more tranquil and appealing setting, try lodging on Castle Hill near Bratislava Castle. This vantage point provides breathtaking views of the city and the Danube River.
- While it is a little out from the busy city centre, it gives a calm respite after a day of travelling and is quite accessible to the Old Town by foot or public transportation.

Pitálska and Apollo Bridge areas:
- This charming neighborhood is known for its contemporary architecture as well as stylish cafés and eateries. It's an excellent option for those who appreciate modern metropolitan environments.
- Because it is well-connected to the rest of the city, the Apollo Bridge region is ideal for touring as well as experiencing local cuisine and nightlife.

Bratislava Forest Park (Lesopark):
- If you're looking for a peaceful and green vacation, staying in Bratislava Forest Park is an excellent option. This location is ideal for nature lovers and outdoor enthusiasts, with hiking trails and breathtaking scenery.
- While it is a little out of the way from the city centre, it provides a peaceful reprieve and an opportunity to see the city's natural beauty.

Each Bratislava area offers a unique experience, and the best one for you will be determined by your interests, budget, and preferred activities. Whether you like the historical beauty of Old Town, the contemporary vibes of Eurovea, or the peace of Castle Hill, Bratislava has a neighbourhood for you.

Hotels and resorts

The Grand Hotel River Park in Bratislava, a Luxury Collection Hotel:
• Address: 6 Dvoákovo nábreie, Bratislava, Slovakia 811 02
• Description: This beautiful five-star hotel along the Danube River offers stunning views and convenient access to the Old Town. The hotel has exquisite rooms, a spa, a fitness centre, and a variety of dining options.
• Prices: Prices vary depending on the kind of accommodation and the time of year.

Boutique Hotel Marrol:
• Address: Tobrucká 4, 811 02 Bratislava, Slovakia
Marrol's Boutique Hotel is a superb and inviting facility in the heart of the city, close to major attractions and retail districts. There is a spa, a library, and a restaurant serving Slovak and foreign cuisine within the hotel.
• Room pricing may vary depending on the room type and season.

Gallery of the Central Lindner Hotel:
• Address: Metodova 4, 821 08 Bratislava, Slovakia
• Description: The Lindner Hotel Gallery Central in New Town offers contemporary and sophisticated

rooms. The hotel has a fitness centre, a rooftop patio, and a variety of dining options.
Rates vary depending on the accommodation type and booking dates.

Mama's Hotel Design & Boutique:
• Address: Laurinská 1, 811 01 Bratislava, Slovakia.
The magnificent and contemporary Mama's Design & Boutique Hotel is located in the heart of Bratislava's Old Town. It has beautiful, one-of-a-kind accommodations, a rooftop patio, and a delightful restaurant serving international cuisine.
• Lodging costs may vary depending on the kind of hotel and the time of year.

The Devin Inn:
• Address: Riecna 4, 811 02 Bratislava, Slovakia
• Description: Located near Bratislava Castle, this four-star hotel offers stunning views of the Danube River. The hotel has spacious rooms, a spa, and a restaurant with a patio.
• Rates: Rates vary depending on room type and season.

Always check the hotels' official websites for the most up-to-date price, availability, and special discounts.

Breakfast at Bed and Breakfast

In contrast to large hotels, B&Bs are typically small, family-run businesses that provide a more personalised and customised accommodation experience. They typically have a pleasant and cosy atmosphere, and the hosts are well-known for their kind hospitality. Breakfast is usually included in B&B stays, giving visitors the choice of starting the day with a prepared meal and local delights.

Many B&Bs in Bratislava are situated in beautiful historic buildings or quiet residential neighbourhoods, allowing visitors to experience the city as a native would. While they may have fewer rooms than larger hotels, B&Bs place an emphasis on comfort, a distinctive setting, and a personal touch that appeals to consumers looking for a more genuine experience.

B&Bs in Bratislava that are popular include:

Please keep in mind that the information in the list below is as of September 2021, and pricing and addresses may have changed after then. Make sure you have the most up-to-date information before making any bookings.

Patio at the hostel:
• Location: Suché mto 6, 811 03 Bratislava, Slovakia Patio Hostel offers both private rooms and dormitory accommodations. The communal areas and pleasant surroundings make it an ideal location for budget travelers.
• Breakfast: Guests may enjoy a continental breakfast in the communal cooking area.

Penzion Berg:
• Address: Zochova 8, 811 03 Bratislava, Slovakia.
• Penzion Berg, located near Bratislava Castle, offers pleasant and relaxing rooms. Because of the location of the B&B, visitors may explore both the city and the neighboring wooded hills.
• Breakfast: A continental breakfast is served each morning.

Penzión Pohodika:
M.R. Tefánika 8, 900 21 Devnska Nová Ves, Slovak Republic
• Description: Penzión Pohodika, located near Devnska Nová Ves, provides a peaceful getaway from the city. The B&B's garden and patio provide a tranquil setting for relaxation.

• Breakfast: A full breakfast is served every day.

Penzion, Vilo:
• Address: Franziska námestie 4, Bratislava, Slovakia 811 01
• Penzion Vilo is a delightful and peaceful stay in a historical building in the heart of Bratislava's Old Town. The B&B's location allows guests easy access to main sights and eating options.
• Breakfast: A superb buffet breakfast is served in the dining room.

Please verify with the B&Bs directly for the most up-to-date price, availability, and addresses. B&Bs in Bratislava are an excellent way to immerse yourself in the city's warmth and unique charm.

Leases on Apartments

Bratislava Apartment Rentals are classified as follows:

Short-term Rentals: These flats are ideal for travelers who need temporary housing. They are typically fully furnished and equipped with basic facilities, making them ideal for quick trips to Bratislava.

Long-term Apartment Rentals: Long-term apartment rentals are intended for individuals or families who plan to stay in Bratislava for an extended period of time. These rentals often require the signing of a lease agreement for a period of several months or more.

Serviced flats combine the convenience of a hotel with the privacy of an apartment. They provide housekeeping, concierge services, and other perks and are suitable for both short and extended visits.

Studio Apartments: Studio apartments are small, self-contained apartments that incorporate a living and sleeping room. They are an excellent choice for single travelers or couples looking for low-cost lodging. Apartments with one, two, or three bedrooms accommodate families or groups by providing separate bedrooms, a living space, and a kitchen or kitchenette. They are larger and more private than hotel rooms.

Upscale luxury flats in Bratislava have premium amenities such as high-end decor, contemporary appliances, and exclusive access to facilities like fitness centers and swimming pools.

Platforms for Finding Bratislava Apartment Rentals:

Airbnb: Airbnb is a popular website for short-term flat rentals, offering a wide range of properties from individual hosts.

Booking.com: In addition to hotels, Booking.com offers flat rentals in Bratislava, enabling you to personalize your search to meet your specific needs.

HomeAway specializes in vacation rentals and offers a variety of flats and vacation houses in Bratislava.

Expats.cz: Expats and foreign students looking for long-term flat rentals in Bratislava should check out this website.

Local Real Estate firms: Local real estate firms in Bratislava can assist you in locating long-term rental options as well as with the necessary paperwork and formalities.

When looking for flat rentals, consider factors like location, closeness to public transit and attractions, amenities, and price. Examine reviews and engage directly with the hosts or property management to confirm that the flat meets your requirements and expectations.

Chapter 5. Top Attractions in Bratislava.

Bratislava Castle

Bratislava Castle, perched majestically on a hill above the charming city of Bratislava, is a symbol of the country's rich history and cultural heritage. During my visit to this old landmark, I was struck by its majesty and the panoramic views it provided.

As I reached the cobblestone lanes leading to the castle's gate, I couldn't help but feel a rush of adrenaline and excitement. The castle's gorgeous white walls and shining towers loomed in front of me, a tribute to the centuries of history that had unfolded beyond its gates.

As I neared the courtyard, I was struck by a sense of timelessness, as if I had been transported back in time. The castle's architecture, a mix of Gothic, Renaissance, and Baroque styles, projected imperial majesty. As I explored the castle's interior, I marvelled at the gorgeous rooms covered with stunning paintings and superb plaster embellishments. Each chamber appeared to tell a story about the royals and nobility who had passed through these passages.

The crown gem of the castle, the Crown Tower, was unquestionably the highlight of my visit. After climbing its spiral staircase, I was rewarded with a stunning view of Bratislava's old town and the Danube River at the summit. The view was stunning, as if the city had revealed its most valuable secrets from this vantage point.

As I stood there, taking in the magnificence of Slovakia's capital set out before me, I felt a great connection to the past and a deeper appreciation for the significance of this old bastion. Bratislava Castle had evolved into more than just a historical landmark; it had become a window into Slovakia's spirit, a tribute to the country's perseverance, culture, and unwavering character.

I sat on a seat in the castle grounds after my visit to reflect on my experience. I was grateful for the chance to view the splendour of Bratislava Castle and the beauty of the city it overlooks. It was a peaceful moment that I will remember.

In my heart, Bratislava Castle will always be a source of astonishment and surprise. It was more than just a beautiful sight to see; it was an event that moved my spirit. As I said goodbye to this magnificent fortress, I realised that my trip to Slovakia will be inextricably linked to the splendour of Bratislava Castle—a timeless monument of a nation's history and a symbol of its eternal heritage.

St. Martin's Cathedral

St. Martin's Cathedral, situated in the heart of Bratislava, Slovakia, is a magnificent architectural masterpiece with significant historical and cultural significance.

This magnificent Gothic cathedral is a testimony to the region's strong spiritual culture, serving as a beacon of faith and perseverance for centuries.

As I approached St. Martin's Cathedral, I was struck by its tall spire and beautiful façade. The façade, which was adorned with stunning sculptures and flawless workmanship, seemed to be telling its own story. The magnificent gateway drew me in, and I entered a spiritual refuge.

The inside of the church exuded seriousness and commitment. As my eyes adjusted to the dim light, I found myself surrounded by towering vaulted ceilings, gorgeous stained glass windows, and intricate altars. The majesty of the nave and the magnificent beauty of the columns astounded me, reminding me of the Gothic era's great workmanship.

One of St. Martin's Cathedral's most compelling features is the astoundingly gorgeous altar, a masterpiece of wood carving and religious symbolism. The beautiful artwork displayed on the altar seemed to come to life, narrating biblical stories and creating a sense of mysticism.

As I strolled inside the church, I saw various chapels, each with its own unique artwork and antiquities. I was captivated by the artistic richness and religious conviction on display in the Chapel of St. Anne, with its wonderful paintings, and the Chapel of St. Stephen, with its gorgeous golden altar.

But climbing the cathedral's tower was arguably the most moving part of my visit. As I climbed the small spiral staircase, the bells chimed softly in the distance, providing a wonderful backdrop to my journey. When I finally made it to the top, I was greeted with a stunning panoramic view of Bratislava. The red-tiled rooftops of the city spread out under me, while the Danube River flowed gently, connecting the past and the present.

From the top of the tower, I had a better understanding of St. Martin's Cathedral's historical significance. Its spire, rising to the skies, seemed to embody the people's hopes, while its foundations, firmly planted in the ground, reflected the city's and its residents' lasting spirit.

As I ascended the tower and said goodbye to St. Martin's Cathedral, I was overcome with peace and gratitude. This house of worship had left an indelible imprint on my mind, a testament to the force of human creation, faith, and the ongoing history of a wonderful city.

St. Martin's Cathedral stands as an eternal reminder of the beauty of human expression as well as the powerful effect that architecture has on the human psyche. It is a time-traveling destination that enables visitors to immerse themselves in the embrace of history, art, and spirituality—a calm refuge in the heart of Bratislava.

The Old Town Hall and Main Square

The Old Town Hall and Main Square in Bratislava are the beating heart of the city's historical and cultural heritage. These landmark sites take visitors back in time, providing a glimpse into Bratislava's glorious history while remaining contemporary.

As I walked through the cobblestone pathways of Old Town, I marveled at the remarkable mix of architectural styles that adorned the buildings around the Main Square. The region's vast breadth and lively spirit provided an exhilarating contrast to the old buildings that surrounded it.

With its unique white tower and beautiful exterior, the Old Town Hall was a striking feature of the plaza. This centuries-old structure has seen the ups and downs of history, serving as the seat of local government and sustaining various alterations throughout the years. Its clock tower, which was adorned with a beautiful golden crown, added to the grandeur of the skyline.

I uncovered a gold mine of historic antiques and displays depicting the growth of Bratislava when I entered the Old Town Hall. The museum inside the hall takes visitors on a fascinating journey through the history of the city, from mediaeval times to the present. Climbing the spiral staircase of the tower provided me with a breathtaking perspective of the Main Square below and the city beyond.

As I walked farther into the Main Square, I discovered a plethora of fantastic cafés, boutique boutiques, and art galleries. The area was a hive of activity, with people and tourists interacting and contributing to the rich fabric of Bratislava's urban life.

The Main Square holds a variety of events and festivals throughout the year, lending energy to its historic ambience. I entered a bustling neighborhood market where merchants proudly displayed their wares, which ranged from homemade gifts to traditional Slovak fare.

The Old Town Hall and Main Square's uniqueness and charm were much more obvious in the evening. As the sun went down, the area transformed into an enchanted world of lit facades and a warm, delightful air. The tower of the town hall shone in the night sky, a beacon of legacy and culture in the heart of modernity.

As I said farewell to the Old Town Hall and Main Square, I was struck by Bratislava's ability to seamlessly blend its old heritage with the pulse of modern life. The historic monuments and lively squares of the city served as a reminder of the importance of preserving a city's heritage.

The Old Town Hall and Main Square have a unique position in the heart of Bratislava, serving not only as symbols of the city's history, but also as coveted places that influence the city's present and future. They are a testament to the tenacity and energy of a city that honor's its past while enjoying the vitality of the present.

Devin's Castle

Devin Castle, perched on a rock overlooking the Danube and Morava rivers, is a stunning tribute to Slovakia's long history and strategic significance. This old castle, shrouded in tales and secrets, looks to be frozen in time, luring visitors on a journey through history.

My journey to Devin Castle started with a leisurely walk along a wonderful route that wound through thick flora and provided views of the Danube River below.

As I reached the castle ruins, the sight of its jagged stone walls against the azure sky astounded and intrigued me.

As I reached the castle grounds, I felt a strong connection to the past. The ruins of mediaeval walls, archways, and watchtowers gave quiet witness to the centuries that had passed behind these walls. The Castle's strategic location above the river valley was obvious, and I could only imagine the wars fought and legends of valour and courage carved in its stones.

Climbing to the top of the castle tower provided me with breathtaking views of the surrounding countryside that stretched far into the distance. The Danube River flowed serenely below, while the Morava River complemented the scene. The confluence of these two rivers seemed to represent the meeting of history and nature, creating a harmonious tapestry of time and beauty.

As I explored the castle's interior, I was drawn to the subterranean tunnels, where hidden rooms and secret corridors mumbled stories of intrigue and mystery. Footsteps seemed to reverberate with voices from the past, thrilling my imagination and inspiring wonder.

Devin Castle boasts stunning natural beauty in addition to historical significance. The surrounding cliffs and lush woods provided a calm hideaway where I could stop and admire nature's beauty with the castle's rustic charm.

My visit to Devin Castle was not just a tour into the past, but also a personal revelation, a reminder of the endurance of the human spirit and the eternal legacy of a nation's history. The castle's ancient stones bore the weight of history, but they also bore witness to the might of human innovation and brilliance.

I left Devin Castle in awe of this hallowed location, where history and nature merged, stories lived on, and echoes of the past connected with the present. Devin Castle is a treasured reminder of a time and magical journey, as well as an everlasting symbol of Slovakia's cultural identity.

UFO Observation Platform

The UFO Observation Deck, located atop the Most SNP Bridge (Bridge of the Slovak National Uprising) in Bratislava, Slovakia, is a futuristic masterpiece that provides a unique and breathtaking view of the city. This extraordinary tower, designed in the shape of a flying saucer, serves as both an observation deck and a symbol of Bratislava's modernism and growth.

My trip to the UFO Observation Deck started with an exhilarating lift journey to the bridge tower's top. As the doors opened, I went out into the circular observation deck, where I was met with spectacular panoramic views of the city and its surroundings.

The vast Danube River flowing through Bratislava was stunning, and the historical splendour of the ancient town contrasted wonderfully with the contemporary city. I could see Bratislava Castle, Devin Castle, and St. Martin's Cathedral from this vantage position, giving me a bird's-eye view of the city's rich cultural history.

The observation deck's wrap-around windows enabled me to take in the city's splendour from every angle, capturing the spirit of Bratislava's unique combination of history and present. The vista was particularly stunning at sunset, when the sky became orange and pink, casting a beautiful glow over the whole city.

While the stunning views were undoubtedly the highlight of the UFO Observation Deck, there was more to discover on the interior. The UFO Restaurant and Bar provided a delectable gourmet journey, with great meals and beverages that added to the overall mood of elegance and refinement.

As the evening progressed, I took use of the deck's Star Deck experience, which had an outside platform where I could feel the cold wind on my skin and stare at the stars. Flying above the city, surrounded by the beautiful lights that adorned Bratislava's skyline, was a fantastic experience.

The UFO Observation Deck is more than just a spot to see Bratislava from above; it's also a place to get a better understanding of the city's growth, embrace of technology, and resolve to reach for the stars. It serves as a reminder that, although preserving history is important, so is embracing innovation and planning for the future.

As I left the UFO Observation Deck, I was overcome with awe and gratitude for having visited such a rare and wonderful location. It was a fantastic trip that allowed me to see Bratislava in a new light and appreciate its many beauties. The UFO Observation Deck is a treasured memento of a really extraordinary event, as well as a distinguishing symbol of Bratislava's goals.

The Bratislava City Museum

The Bratislava City Museum, situated in the heart of Slovakia's capital, is a treasure trove of historical and cultural artefacts that take visitors on an interesting journey through the city's history. The museum is housed inside the majestic Old Town Hall, a historical monument that adds to the authenticity of the presentations.

My visit to the Bratislava City Museum started with a kind greeting from the staff, who were eager to share the city's rich history with tourists. As soon as I stepped inside, I was immersed in a world of ancient treasures, historical documents, and spectacular exhibitions depicting Bratislava's development from prehistoric to present times.

The museum's exceptional collection of archaeological artefacts from various ages, which provided information on the early communities that once flourished on the Danube River's banks, was one of its main draws. The exhibitions of Roman antiquities and mediaeval artefacts emphasised the strategic significance of the city as a crossroads of civilizations and commerce networks.

The museum's attention to detail and interactive exhibits enhanced the time travel journey. I was transported back in time as I walked through wonderfully recreated ancient rooms, watching the everyday life of Bratislava's previous inhabitants.

The exhibit on the Slovak National Uprising, a significant event in the city's history, piqued my interest in particular. The museum used images, personal accounts, and actual artefacts to remember the bravery and sacrifices of those who fought for freedom and independence during World War II.

The museum's art collection includes works by well-known Slovakian artists, demonstrating the country's creative prowess and aesthetic legacy.

In addition to its permanent displays, the Bratislava City Museum hosts a variety of temporary exhibitions, cultural events, and educational activities, making it a dynamic and developing place that provides something new with each visit.

As I walked through the museum's corridors, I couldn't help but be grateful for the efforts to preserve and promote Bratislava's distinct character and tradition. The Bratislava City

Museum is more than just a museum; it is a place where the city's history is brought to life, stories are shared, and the city's journey is treasured and remembered.

I left the Bratislava City Museum with a better understanding of the city's history and a renewed appreciation for its cultural assets. The museum had stayed with me, enhancing my experience of Bratislava and inspiring pride in the city's incredible past. It was a journey through time that I would cherish as a cherished memory of my time in this enchanting city.

Slavin's Memorial

The Slavin Memorial, perched atop a hill overlooking Bratislava, is a solemn and moving tribute to the brave soldiers who gave their lives during World War II for the city's liberation, and it holds a special place in the hearts of the people of Bratislava, serving as a symbol of remembrance, gratitude, and national pride.

As I made my way up the hill towards Slavin Memorial, I was struck by how calm and serene the surroundings were. The well-kept gardens and rows of graves exuded dignity and respect, creating a solemn but peaceful atmosphere.

When I arrived to the memorial, I was met by a gigantic obelisk and a big colonnade, both adorned with sculptures and inscriptions honouring the fallen soldiers. The centre bronze sculpture depicts a soldier standing tall and determined, representing the bravery and sacrifice of Slovakian forces fighting for freedom and independence.

The view from the Slavin Memorial was spectacular, with a panoramic view of Bratislava below. The city's red-tiled rooftops and old monuments seemed to celebrate those who had given their lives to ensure the city's future.

I found a calm and meditative spot within the monument's tomb—a refuge of thought and devotion. The names of the troops buried here are engraved in stone, serving as a sad reminder of their sacrifice and devotion to their motherland.

While the Slavin Memorial honours those who fought in WWII, it is also a place of connection and healing. It is a monument to the human spirit's resilience and memory's ability to transcend historical divides and unite people in the pursuit of peace and freedom.

As I walked away from the Slavin Memorial, I felt a strong sense of humility and gratitude for the sacrifices made by the warriors who protected Bratislava's liberty. The monument left an unforgettable imprint on my heart, reminding me of the importance of liberty, peace, and togetherness.

The Slavin Memorial is both a terrible reminder of the past and a beacon of hope for the future—a place where heroes' legacies live on and the spirit of the people of Bratislava is inextricably linked with the history of those who strove for a better world. It is a place where we may remember, reflect on, and honour the bravery and sacrifice of those who gave their lives for the love of their country.

Chapter 6. Investigating the Historic District.

A Walking Tour of Old Town

As the sun rose and sent a warm light over the cobblestone pathways of Bratislava's Old Town, I went on a walking tour that promised to reveal the city's hidden gems and rich history. As a knowledgeable guide guided the way, I felt a sense of excitement and anticipation, eager to immerse myself in the tales of the past.

Our adventure began at the magnificent Michael's Gate, one of Bratislava's few intact mediaeval gates. I stood under its historic arch, admiring its wonderful features and imagining the many visitors who had passed through its gates throughout the years. Our guide told us fascinating stories about the gate's importance as a symbol of the city's power and perseverance.

As we walked through the lovely streets, the guide pointed out historical sites and architectural marvels, bringing the Old Town's story to life. The pastel-colored façade and Baroque-style buildings exuded old-world beauty, but the vibrant cafés and businesses added a contemporary touch.

We made our way to Main Square, where the Old Town Hall's massive tower dominated the area. I learnt about the hall's transformation from an administrative centre to a museum, as well as its significance in preserving Bratislava's cultural heritage. The panoramic view of the town from the tower's summit was breathtaking, and I felt a strong connection to Bratislava's history and present.

Our tour guide took us to St. Martin's Cathedral, a magnificent Gothic structure that houses centuries of history. As soon as I stepped inside, I was drawn to the grandeur of the interior, which was adorned with gorgeous stained glass windows and complex sculptures. The guide told fascinating stories of coronations and royal festivities that had taken place in this hallowed place.

While walking around the Old Town, we came upon the majestic Primate's Palace, an architectural marvel that exuded elegance and beauty. The Hall of Mirrors took my breath away with its gorgeous artworks and dazzling chandeliers. I could almost imagine the nobles and nobility who had frequented this magnificent theatre in the past.

Our journey concluded in the gorgeous Hviezdoslav Square, named for the well-known Slovak poet. The plaza's open area and unique vibe drew both residents and tourists. As I said my goodbyes to my guide and the other tour participants, I was overcome with gratitude for the wonderful experience.

The walking tour of Bratislava's Old Town not only provided an insightful look into the city's past, but also helped me connect with its soul—the essence of a city that values its history while welcoming growth and change. I travelled through the pages of Bratislava's history, becoming more conscious of its cultural heritage and the personalities who shaped its narrative with each step.

As I walked through the scenic alleys of Old Town again, I carried with me the memories of the walking tour—a voyage that had left an indelible impression on my heart and sparked a desire to learn more about this great city's rich history and culture. Bratislava's Old Town had enchanted me, and I knew I'd remember this exhilarating walking tour for the rest of my life.

Historic sites and architecture

Slovakia's capital, Bratislava, has a rich tapestry of monuments and architectural masterpieces that reflect the country's diversified history and cultural heritage. The architecture of the city is a wonderful combination of old and modern, ranging from mediaeval fortifications to stately homes and modern monuments.

Bratislava Castle is one of the city's most famous monuments, perched majestically on a hill above the city. This majestic stronghold, with its distinctive four-cornered design and white façade, is a reminder of the city's heritage and strategic significance as a centre of power and authority.

St. Martin's Cathedral is another major landmark that dominates the city's skyline. With its towering spire and exquisite workmanship, this imposing Gothic cathedral pays homage to Bratislava's religious legacy as well as the historical importance of the place where Hungarian emperors were coronated.

The Old Town Hall, situated in the heart of the Old Town, is a magnificent specimen of Renaissance architecture. Its attractive façade and spectacular tower make it a popular destination for those interested in exploring and learning about the city's history.

The Blue Church, also known as St. Elizabeth's Church, is notable for its striking blue facade and Art Nouveau architecture. This one-of-a-kind architectural marvel is popular with both locals and tourists, enthralling visitors with its unusual look.

Aside from historical sites, Bratislava has a plethora of superb examples of contemporary architecture. The SNP Bridge, sometimes known as the "UFO Bridge," has a spectacular flying saucer-shaped observation deck with sweeping city views. This magnificent structure exemplifies Bratislava's affluence and modernity.

The Slovak Radio Building, with its remarkable inverted pyramid shape, is another superb contemporary architectural gem. This magnificent structure represents the city's willingness to embrace modern architecture and innovation.

Bratislava's architecture reflects both the city's rich history and its promising future. The vistas and architecture of the city tell the story of its evolution through time, from mediaeval defences and ancient palaces to contemporary wonders.

Exploring Bratislava's architecture is like going through time, where ancient buildings and new concepts coexist. It is a city where history and creativity collide, resulting in a beautiful urban setting that dazzles visitors with the beauty of human creation and the lasting spirit of a city that moves forward while honouring its past.

Restaurants, coffee shops, and bars

Cafes:
• Urban House: Located in the city centre, Urban House is known for its stylish and modern atmosphere. Coffee and pastries often cost between €2 and €5. Michalská 3, 811 01 Bratislava is the address.

• Mondieu Bistro: This lovely café in the Old Town offers coffee and desserts for €2.50 to €6. The address is Panenská 5, 811 03 Bratislava.

• Kava.Bar: A specialised coffee store offering a wide range of high-quality coffees. Specialty coffees may range in price from €2.50 to €5. 811 03 Bratislava, Slovakia, Panenská 682/30.

Restaurants:
• Slovak Pub: Slovak Pub, located in the heart of Old Town, serves traditional Slovak cuisine. Prices for main courses typically vary from €8 to €15. 811 06 Bratislava, Slovakia, Obchodná 620/62.

• Flagship: A modern European restaurant that serves great cuisine. Dinners might range between €15 and €30. Eurovea can be found at Pribinova 8, 811 09 Bratislava.

• Bratislavsk Metiansky Pivovar: This restaurant and brewery serves Slovak cuisine as well as a wide selection of beers. Main courses are typically priced between €10 and €20. The address is Drevená 8, 811 06 Bratislava.

Bars:
• UFO Bar: Located atop the SNP Bridge, the UFO Bar provides spectacular views. Drinks typically cost between €5 and €10. Most SNP, Bratislava, 851 01 Slovakia.

• Subclub: Known for its subterranean vibe, Subclub provides an unforgettable experience. The cost of admission and refreshments varies depending on the event. The address is Nábreie arm. gen. L. Svobodu, 811 02 Bratislava.

• Nu Spirit Bar: A one-of-a-kind and artistic bar with drink prices ranging from €6 to €10. The address is Medená 16, 811 02 Bratislava.

Please keep in mind that this is just a small selection of Bratislava's eating and nightlife options; there are many more cafés, restaurants, and pubs to discover. It's usually a good idea to look into local reviews and suggestions to find locations that fit your hobbies and tastes.

Chapter 7. Bratislava's Culinary Scene.

Traditional Slovak Cuisine

Traditional Slovak food is a potent and delectable representation of the country's rich culinary tradition, with recipes handed down from generation to generation. Slovak cuisine, which is based on Central European and Slavic traditions, includes a variety of dishes made using locally produced ingredients, emphasising the region's verdant fields' richness.

Bryndzové Haluky: Known as Slovakia's national dish, Bryndzové Haluky is a filling and satisfying supper. Small potato dumplings called 'haluky' are drowned in a creamy sheep cheese sauce called 'bryndza', which is flavoured with chunks of fried bacon or sausage. This supper is a must-try for anybody looking for authentic Slovak flavours.

Kapustnica is a traditional Slovak sauerkraut soup given at Christmas and other special occasions. It's made with sauerkraut, dried mushrooms, smoked sausage and a variety of spices, yielding a strong and sour taste that warms the soul, particularly in the winter.

Pirohy: Pirohy in Slovakia are dumplings filled with a variety of fillings, similar to pierogi in other Central and Eastern European nations. Fillings often used include potatoes, cottage cheese, meat, and fruits. They are often fried and served with butter, sour cream, or bacon.

Segedin Goulash (Segednsk Gulá): This unique goulash is made with pig or veal, sauerkraut, onions, and a generous amount of paprika. It's often eaten with dumplings or bread, and the combination of delicate pork and acidic sauerkraut creates a delectable culinary balance.

Loke (Thin Potato Pancakes): Loke are thin potato pancakes that are usually served as a side dish or dessert. They go well with both savoury toppings like goose fat and sour cream and sweet fillings like poppy seeds or jam.

Slovak potato pancakes made with shredded potatoes, flour, and spices are known as Zemiakové Placky. They may be served as a main course or as a side dish with sour cream or applesauce after being pan-fried till golden brown.

Parenica: A characteristic Slovak sheep cheese, Parenica is a smoked cheese with a distinct texture and taste. It is typically taken with bread or used in a variety of cuisines to add flavour to the meal.

Trdelnik: Despite not being a native of Slovakia, Trdelnik has become a beloved sweet delicacy in the country. It is a rolling pastry made of dough that has been grilled over an open fire, sugared, and occasionally filled with Nutella, ice cream, or other toppings.

Slovak cuisine values the simplicity and purity of its ingredients, reflecting the country's deep connection to its agricultural background. Whether you visit small local cafés or take part in traditional Slovak festivals, the country's food will leave an indelible impression with its amazing flavour and heartfelt feasts.

Must-Try Dishes and Drinks

There are some must-try foods and beverages in Slovakia that highlight the country's rich flavour and traditional culinary pleasures. From hearty feasts to sweet treats and refreshing beverages, here are some must-try meals and drinks in Slovakia:

Bryndzové Haluky: As previously said, Bryndzové Haluky is a must-try national dish of Slovakia. The soft potato dumplings are smothered with creamy sheep cheese (bryndza) and topped with fried bacon or sausage to create a delightful combination of textures and tastes.

Kapustnica: This savoury sauerkraut soup is a traditional Slovak Christmas meal, but it's also enjoyed on special occasions all year. The combination of sauerkraut, dried mushrooms, smoked sausage and spices is unexpected and delicious.

Pirohy: Pirohy are Slovak dumplings with a range of sweet and savoury fillings. Whether filled with potatoes, cottage cheese, meat, or fruits, these dumplings provide a diverse and delicious gourmet experience.

Loke are thin potato pancakes that are popular in Slovakia as a side dish or dessert. They are commonly served with savoury toppings such as goose fat or sour cream, as well as sweet fillings such as poppy seeds or jam.

Haluky s Kyslou Kapustou: A haluky variety, this meal consists of potato dumplings served with sour fermented cabbage (kyslá kapusta) and is often accompanied with smoked pig or sausages.

Zemiakové Placky: In many Slovak households, these crispy potato pancakes are eaten as a side dish or snack with sour cream.

Segedin Goulash (Segednsk Gulá): A delicious and tangy meal made with pig or veal stewed with sauerkraut and a generous amount of paprika.

Demänovka: A well-known herbal liqueur made from a combination of herbs, Demänovka is typically used as a digestive or aperitif.

Slovak Wine: Slovakia has a rich history of winemaking, and wine enthusiasts should try some of the country's wines. Riesling, Grüner Veltliner, and Frankovka (Blaufränkisch) are among the notable grape varieties grown in the nation.

Tatransky caj: While visiting the High Tatras area, try Tatransky caj, a hot tea flavoured with alcohol.

It's ideal for warming up after a day of mountain hiking.

Medovina is a sweet and fragrant fermented honey-based alcoholic beverage. It is also referred to as honey wine or mead. It is a traditional drink with historical significance in Slovakia.

These dishes and beverages highlight Slovakia's culinary heritage and cultural diversity. Exploring the flavours of Slovak food, whether indulging in savoury haluky or sipping on local wines, is an important component of any visit to this beautiful and varied nation.

Popular restaurants and grocery stores

Popular Restaurants:
Slovak Pub: Slovak Pub, located in the heart of Old Town, is a well-known restaurant known for its authentic Slovak food. It has a friendly and rustic atmosphere that appeals to both residents and visitors.

Flagship is a modern European restaurant in Eurovea that focuses on high-quality ingredients and unique cuisine. It's an excellent option for those looking for a more sophisticated gourmet experience.

This stylish city centre cafe serves a wide variety of foreign and Slovak meals. It's a popular spot for breakfast, lunch, and casual dining.

Modra Hviezda: Nestled in the majesty of Bratislava Castle's gardens, Modra Hviezda offers a superb dining experience with breathtaking views. It serves traditional Slovak dishes with a contemporary twist.

Metiansky Pivovar is a prominent restaurant and brewery in the historical centre that serves traditional Slovak food and a variety of specialty brews.

Food Shops:
Bratislava Old Market Hall: This gourmet attraction was built in the early twentieth century. Here you may find stalls selling fresh fruit, local cheeses, meats, and traditional Slovak pastries.

Stará Trnica (Old Market): This open-air market holds a variety of events, including farmers' markets, flea markets, and gourmet festivals. It's a great place to eat local street cuisine and buy fresh fruits and veggies.

Trhovisko Miletiova: This massive outdoor market sells fresh fruits and vegetables, meats, dairy products, and other essentials. It's a local favourite because to its low prices and wide selection of regional items.

Fresh Market (Trhovisko Bratislava): Located in the Petralka area, this market is a bustling marketplace for fresh fruits, vegetables, and other regional items.

Farmárske Trhy (Farmers' Market): Held on weekends at several locations across the city, the Farmers' Market brings together local producers and sells organic vegetables, handcrafted goods, and homemade sweets.

These noteworthy restaurants and food markets represent just a small portion of the countless gourmet options available in Bratislava. Exploring the city's eating scene is an exciting way to immerse yourself in Slovakian culture and food, whether you're looking for traditional Slovak delicacies or cosmopolitan flavours.

Chapter 8. Purchasing in Bratislava

Best Shopping Districts

Bratislava has a variety of retail districts, each with its own distinct personality and selection of businesses, making it a popular shopping destination. Here are some of the greatest retail areas in Bratislava:

Obchodná Street: Obchodná Street, located in the city centre, is a popular retail street in Bratislava. This pedestrian-friendly district is densely packed with shops, boutiques, and department stores selling a variety of clothing, accessories, electronics, and other things. It is an excellent location for both domestic and foreign businesses.

Eurovea is a contemporary commercial and leisure complex on the Danube River. This upscale shopping centre is home to a range of retailers, including fashion labels, beauty shops, and specialty businesses. Eurovea also has a number of restaurants, cafés, and a cinema, making it an ideal location for a day of shopping and entertainment.

Aupark: Another famous shopping mall in Bratislava, Aupark offers a diverse range of retail options. With approximately 200 shops, it caters to a wide range of interests and inclinations. Apart from shopping, visitors may enjoy a variety of cuisine options as well as entertainment options such as a theatre and a bowling alley.

Avion Shopping Park: Located near Bratislava Airport, Avion Shopping Park is a large retail mall with a mix of foreign and local businesses. It's an excellent option for fashion, home goods, technology, and other necessities.

SNP Square: This large plaza in Old Town is often home to outdoor markets, like as traditional artisan fairs and seasonal markets. It's a great place to look for local handicrafts, souvenirs, and other one-of-a-kind items.

Stará Trnica (Old Market): In addition to food markets, Stará Trnica (Old Market) hosts design and crafts events on a regular basis, where visitors may discover handcrafted handicrafts, jewellery, and other creative works.

Incheba Expo is primarily an exposition and event centre, although it also hosts a variety of retail events and fairs throughout the year. Visitors may investigate fashion, design, and other specialty markets.

Bratislava's Christmas Markets: During the holidays, Bratislava's Christmas markets take the stage, transforming the city into a winter paradise. Handicrafts, Christmas decorations, regional specialties, and warming drinks are available at these winter markets.

These shopping malls in Bratislava provide a diverse and enjoyable retail experience. The city caters to a wide range of interests and prices, from sophisticated shopping malls to traditional markets, making it an ideal location for retail therapy and cultural discovery via shopping.

Souvenirs and regional crafts

Bratislava has a fantastic selection of local crafts and souvenirs depicting the city's rich cultural history and customs. Here are some must-buy Bratislava local crafts and souvenirs, ranging from traditional handicrafts to one-of-a-kind keepsakes:

Traditional Slovak ceramics and pottery are popular presents that serve as both attractive and functional keepsakes. On handmade ceramic mugs, plates, bowls, and decorative objects, look for fascinating folk motifs and designs.

Wooden Products: Because Slovakia has a long tradition of woodworking, you may find a wide variety of wooden souvenirs, including hand-carved figures, household goods, and exquisite wooden boxes covered with Slovak folk themes.

Slovak glassmaking is well-known, and beautiful glassware and crystal items may be found in Bratislava. Consider carrying beautiful glass decorations, flowers, or traditional Slovak crystal wine glasses home with you.

Traditional blue patterned textiles, known as "modrotlac," are an important part of Slovak culture. These fabrics are used to make a variety of textiles, including scarves, tablecloths, and ornamental items.

Corn Husk Crafts: Corn husk crafts are unique to Slovakia. Among the artistically woven artefacts available are dolls, necklaces, and baskets made from dried maize husks.

Consider buying a small replica of a classic Slovak folk costume, which often includes a neatly embroidered blouse, vest, and skirt, as a great souvenir.

Painted Easter Eggs: Also known as "kraslice," colourful Easter eggs are an important part of Slovak Easter traditions. These eggs have been hand-painted in vibrant colours and themes.

Slovakia is well-known for its spirits and liqueurs, such as slivovica (plum brandy), borovika (juniper brandy), and medovina (honey wine). These are excellent presents or keepsakes for friends and family who want to experience the tastes of Slovakia.

Slovakian honey and honey products are well-known for their exceptional quality and variety of flavour. Look for locally produced honey or honey-infused products such as confectionary and cosmetics.

CDs of Slovak Folk Music and Crafts: Learn more about Slovakia's customs and traditions by collecting traditional folk music CDs or craft-related publications.

When looking for local crafts and gifts in Bratislava, consider visiting the city's Old Town, Christmas markets (during the holiday season), and specialty stores that promote Slovak handcrafted items. These presents not only create treasured memories, but they also benefit local artisans and help to maintain Slovak customs for future generations.

Shopping malls and boutiques.

Bratislava has a diverse assortment of shopping malls and shops that appeal to a wide range of interests and preferences, providing a pleasurable shopping experience for both tourists and locals. Here are some of the most popular shopping centres and stores in the city:

Shopping Malls:
Eurovea: Eurovea is a sophisticated retail and leisure complex along the Danube River that includes a wide range of businesses, restaurants, and recreational facilities. It sells both worldwide and local brands, making it a one-stop shop for clothing, accessories, gadgets, and other items. The complex's riverside promenade provides

breathtaking views that improve the whole shopping experience.

Aupark: With over 200 stores, restaurants, and entertainment options, Aupark is one of Bratislava's main shopping districts. It sells everything from clothing and cosmetics to technology and household goods. The facility is ideal for families, since it has a special children's play area as well as a movie complex.

Central: The Central retail mall, located in the city centre, is a contemporary facility that combines shopping with entertainment and gourmet options. It has a great mix of large worldwide brands and local shops, making it an excellent choice for fashionistas.

Avion Shopping Park: Avion Shopping Park, located near Bratislava Airport, is a large mall with a diverse selection of businesses and restaurants. Avion caters to a wide range of requirements and budgets, from fashion and footwear to electronics and home goods.

Polus City Centre: Polus City Centre, another well-known retail attraction in Bratislava, offers a mix of shopping, eating, and entertainment. The mall is home to well-known fashion retailers, a supermarket, and a theatre complex, making it an ideal place for all-around shopping and leisure.

Boutiques and specialty stores:
Bratislava Old Town: The old town is full with lovely shops and specialty enterprises selling one-of-a-kind and locally manufactured items. Exploring the Old Town's small lanes reveals a bounty of one-of-a-kind items ranging from handcrafted jewellery and art to traditional crafts and souvenirs.

Bratislava has a thriving design culture, with several boutique shops showing modern Slovak designs and trends. These stores provide a carefully curated selection of clothing, accessories, and home décor handcrafted by local craftsmen.

Traditional Craft Shops: Traditional Slovak crafts are preserved and promoted in shops across the city. Handcrafted items such as pottery, woodwork crafts, and folk art are sold at these shops.

Antique businesses: There are many magnificent antique shops in Bratislava that offer unique and historical items ranging from furniture and artwork to unusual souvenirs.

bookshops: Bratislava has a vibrant literary culture, with several bookstores selling books in a variety of languages, including English, as well as Slovak literature and journals.

Bratislava's shopping malls and boutiques provide something for everyone, whether you're looking for the latest fashion trends, locally-made crafts, or one-of-a-kind purchases. From modern shopping malls to little shops, you'll have a great time shopping in Slovakia's vibrant city.

Chapter 9. Outdoor Activities and Nature.

Bratislava Forest Park

Bratislava Forest Park, also known as Bratislavske Lesy Park or simply "Lesopark," is a wonderful green refuge nestled on the foothills of the Small Carpathians, only a short distance from the congested city centre of Bratislava. With an area of approximately 27 square kilometres, it is one of Europe's largest urban forest parks and a popular recreational destination for both residents and tourists.

Attractions and features include:
Bratislava Forest Park is crisscrossed by a network of well-marked walking routes, making it an ideal location for nature lovers and hikers. The paths wind through a variety of environments, from deep woods to meadows, and provide breathtaking views of the city and surrounding area.

The famous Kamzik TV Tower is located in the centre of the forest park and is a renowned landmark offering panoramic views of Bratislava and the surrounding area. A magnificent stroll or the funicular train may take visitors to the pinnacle, where a spinning restaurant awaits.

Animal Enclosures: The forest park has various animal enclosures where visitors may observe and learn about natural creatures. These enclosures provide a safe haven for wild animals like as deer, mouflons, and wild boars.

Picnics, cycling, and horseback riding are among the outdoor activities available in the Bratislava Forest Park. During the warmer months, families and friends gather here to enjoy the scenery and fresh air.

Bratislava Zoo: Another popular destination for families and animal lovers is the Bratislava Zoo, which is located close the woodland park. The zoo contains a wide variety of animals from all over the globe and provides a relaxing day in the middle of nature.

Bratislava Forest Park, in addition to its natural splendour, offers a tranquil location for leisure and recreation. Visitors may come upon peaceful places to rest, meditate, or read a book while listening to the soothing sounds of nature.

Bunker B-S 4: History buffs may visit Bunker B-S 4, a WWII-era bunker situated inside the park. Guided tours provide information about the bunker's historical significance and usefulness during the fight.

Accessibility:
Bratislava Forest Park is a popular day trip or weekend adventure destination since it is easily accessible from the city centre. Public transit, including buses and the funicular train that links the city to Kamzk Hill, provides access to the park.

Bratislava Forest Park is the city's beautiful green lung, providing a remarkable mix of nature, history, and recreational opportunities. The forest park has something for everyone, whether you're looking for adventure on the hiking trails, panoramic views from the Kamzik Tower, or a peaceful retreat into nature.

River cruises on the Danube

Danube River Cruises are an excellent way to view Europe's second-longest river's stunning vistas, historic towns, and charming villages. The Danube River passes through ten countries, including Germany, Austria, Slovakia, Hungary, Serbia,

Croatia, Bulgaria, Romania, Moldova, and Ukraine, making it an ideal route for river cruises with diverse itineraries and experiences.

Danube River Cruise Highlights include:

Scenic Beauty: A Danube cruise provides breathtaking views of undulating hills, vineyards, historic castles, and lovely towns. The river meanders through magnificent landscape during the journey, providing travellers with a stunning and ever-changing background.

Passengers on Danube River Cruises visit historical towns and cultural centres such as Vienna, Budapest, Bratislava, and Belgrade. Tourists may take shore excursions to see architectural marvels, historic landmarks, and museums that highlight the region's rich history and culture.

Culinary Delights: Because the Danube flows through multiple nations, river cruise passengers may sample a variety of cuisines. Guests may sample regional specialties, local wines, and traditional cuisine that represent the unique aspects of each port of call.

River cruises move at a leisurely speed, enabling guests to unwind while admiring the breathtaking scenery. Aboard features include comfortable accommodations, gourmet dining, entertainment, and spa facilities.

Cultural Immersion: Many Danube River Cruises offer themed itineraries centred on art, music, wine, or history. Passengers may learn more about the region's culture by taking part in enrichment events such as talks, food demonstrations, and live performances.

River cruises often include guided shore excursions that let tourists to experience the cities and villages along the Danube. These excursions often include visits to prominent sites, museums, local markets, and off-the-beaten-path treasures.

Flexibility: Depending on your interests and time constraints, you may choose between short tours focusing on certain places and longer adventures including many countries. Cruises may last anything from a few days to many weeks.

Seasonal Attractions: Each season brings with it its own set of attractions to the Danube. Spring gives lovely scenery, while summer delivers comfortable patio dining. Autumn delivers beautiful foliage, while January brings charming Christmas markets.

The experience will be fantastic whether you choose a short city-focused cruise or a thorough Danube River tour. Danube river cruises provide an exceptional combination of leisure, cultural exploration, and scenic splendour, making them a popular option for those seeking a memorable and immersive European experience.

Hiking and biking trails

Hiking and bicycle enthusiasts will be able to appreciate the beautiful scenery around Bratislava. The region's trails vary from peaceful pathways along the Danube River to strenuous treks in the nearby Small Carpathians. The following are some of the most popular hiking and cycling trails in and around Bratislava:

Hiking Trails:

Devin Castle walk:
• Difficulty: Easy
• Time commitment: Approximately 1-2 hours

This well-known walk goes to Devin Castle, a mediaeval fortress built on a rock overlooking the Danube and Morava Rivers. The walk provides panoramic views of the surrounding region and the confluence of the rivers. It's an excellent option for history buffs and families looking for a quick, uncomplicated trek.

Hiking to Kamzik TV Tower:
• Level of Difficulty: Moderate to Easy
• Time required: around 2-3 hours

• The road leads to Kamzk Hill, which is home to the famous Kamzik TV Tower. The climb begins in the city and continues into the wooded hills, with wonderful views of Bratislava from the summit. The trail is well-marked and suitable for both walkers and cyclists.

The hike from Zochova Chata to Pajtn Castle is as follows:
• Moderate Difficulty Level
• Travel time: 4-5 hours (round trip)

This breathtaking journey begins in Zochova Chata, a small hamlet in the Small Carpathians. The walk leads to Pajtn Castle, a dilapidated mediaeval fortress with spectacular views of the surrounding area. The route covers some hilly places, making it an appealing excursion for nature lovers.

Cycling Routes:

Bike Path Along the Danube River:
• Difficulty: Easy
The Danube River Cycling path follows the Danube River through Bratislava, offering a picturesque path for cyclists of all abilities. Beautiful river views may be seen while passing by sites such as the UFO Tower and the Eurovea retail complex. Longer rides are possible since the track continues both upstream and downstream.

Cycling Route in Vydrica:
• Moderate Difficulty Level
The Vydrica Cycling Trail begins in the city centre and winds through the lovely Vydrica neighbourhood. The route travels across urban and nature settings, passing via Bratislava Castle and along the Danube River. It's a fun tour that will teach you about Bratislava's history and culture.

Routes for Cycling in the Carpathians:
• Level of Difficulty: Moderate to Difficult
The Small Carpathians include a network of bike paths that go through vineyards, woodlands, and

charming towns. These are more difficult routes with steep ascents and descents that are best suited to experienced mountain bikers. The effort is rewarded by stunning landscape and a true sense of adventure.

Before embarking on any hiking or cycling journey, it is critical to assess route conditions, pack appropriate clothing, and have adequate water and food. Consider taking a guided tour or joining a local cycling or hiking club for a more enjoyable and safe experience on more difficult routes or longer outings. The beautiful paths of Bratislava provide an enthralling journey through nature and history, highlighting the region's natural beauty and cultural heritage.

Bratislava Zoo and Botanical Garden.

The Bratislava Zoo and Botanical Garden offers tourists a once-in-a-lifetime chance to immerse themselves in the wonders of nature and animals. These lovely Danube River banks provide a welcome escape from the city's hustle and bustle. The following information is provided in full for the Bratislava Zoo and Botanical Garden:

Bratislava Zoo:

The Bratislava Zoo, often known as ZOO Bratislava, is a well-kept zoological park that houses a diverse range of animal species. The primary goals of the zoo are conservation and education, and visitors may learn about animals and environmental preservation.

Among the highlights are:

Animal Exhibits: The zoo is home to about 150 different animal species, including enormous cats, monkeys, reptiles, birds, and others. It provides the animals with a huge, well-designed house that ensures their well-being and natural activities.

Children's Zoo: At ZOO Bratislava, there is a Children's Zoo where young visitors may interact with farm animals and learn about animal care and chores.

DinoPark: A one-of-a-kind DinoPark inside the zoo brings visitors back to the dinosaur era. The life-size replicas of these ancient species appeal to both children and adults.

Animal Feeding Sessions and Demonstrations: The zoo has regular feeding sessions and demonstrations that allow visitors to interact with the animals while learning about their habits and diets.

Environmental Education: The ZOO Bratislava is a valuable resource for increasing awareness of animal conservation and environmental issues. It organises educational programmes and activities to promote animal welfare and environmentally responsible practises.

Bratislava Botanical Garden:
The Bratislava Botanical Garden, also known as Botanická záhrada UK, is a tranquil oasis in the city that displays a wide range of plant species from various climates and locations.

Among the highlights are:
Greenhouses with Themes: The botanical park features a number of greenhouses that replicate diverse climatic zones, including tropical, subtropical, and desert ecosystems. Exotic flora from all around the world may be learned about by visitors.

The Alpine House houses plants found in high-altitude environments, showcasing a varied spectrum of alpine vegetation.

The tranquil Japanese Garden offers a calming atmosphere with traditional Japanese gardening qualities, giving a delightful refuge from the city's turmoil.

Seasonal displays: Throughout the year, the botanical garden's exhibits change to showcase seasonal flowers and plant species. Both the Bratislava Zoo and the Botanical Garden are conveniently accessible by public transportation. They provide enjoyable experiences for visitors of all ages, whether they are interested in animals, plant life, or just wish to spend a relaxing day in the beauty of nature. These places illustrate Bratislava's commitment to conservation, education, and the preservation of biodiversity.

Chapter 10. Nightlife and Entertainment.

Pubs and Nightclubs.

Bratislava's nightlife culture is vibrant and busy, with a variety of clubs and bars scattered around the city. Bratislava has something for everyone, whether you want to drink local beers in a charming pub or a modern bar with creative drinks. The following is a list of the city's bars and pubs:

Taverns in Slovak Tradition:

Slovak Pub:
• Address: Obchodná 62, 811 06 Bratislava, Slovakia
The Slovak Pub is a renowned destination for authentic Slovak food and beer. The rural setting and traditional delicacies, such as bryndzové haluky (dumplings with sheep cheese), make it a favourite among both locals and tourists.

Mr. Richard Jakub:
• Contact information: Venturska 5, 811 01 Bratislava, Slovak Republic.

Richtár Jakub is a trendy but relaxed tavern that caters to beer enthusiasts. It is well-known for its extensive selection of craft beers. It's a great place to try new tastes from a changing lineup of local and foreign brewers.

Cocktail Lounges and Upscale Bars:

The City House:
• Address: 14 Laurinská, Bratislava, Slovakia 811 01
• Urban House is a hip and stylish pub with an industrial vibe. It offers an inventive selection of drinks, artisan beers, and wines, as well as live music and DJ events.

Sky Bar
• Address: 7 Sedlárska, Bratislava, Slovakia 811 01
The Sky Bar, located above the historic Carlton Hotel, offers stunning views of the metropolis and iconic buildings in Bratislava. It's ideal for sunset drinks and gazing at the city lights.

Restaurants Serving Craft Beer:

BeerGeek's Bar:
• Address: 52 Obchodná, Bratislava, Slovakia 811 06
• BeerGeek Bar is a beer lover's paradise, serving a diverse selection of craft beers from Slovakia and

beyond. Professional people may assist you in examining their many alternatives.

BeAbout:
• Location: Panenská 27, 811 03 Bratislava, Slovakia
• BeAbout is a bustling craft beer bar with a diverse tap list including local and international beers. The quiet and pleasant environment appeals to both locals and visitors.

Live Music and Entertainment in Bars:

KC Dunaj:
• Address: 3 Nedbalova, Bratislava, Slovakia 811 01
KC Dunaj is a cultural centre that hosts live music concerts, film screenings, and art exhibits. It's a creative hotspot and an excellent place to discover Bratislava's alternative culture.

The Nu Spirit Lounge and Bar:
• Location: Medená 16, 811 02 Bratislava, Slovakia
• Nu Spirit Bar & Lounge is a well-known establishment known for its DJ sets, live music performances, and themed events. It's a popular hangout for music fans and a lively spot to dance the night away.

As with any other nightlife scene, it is essential to exercise prudence and drink responsibly while enjoying Bratislava's clubs and pubs. If you're looking for a taste of traditional Slovak culture, an intriguing craft beer variety, or a trendy area to relax, Bratislava's bars and pubs provide something for everyone.

Nightclubs and music venues

Bratislava's nightlife comes alive after dark, with a plethora of nightclubs and music venues catering to a broad range of interests and inclinations. From pounding dance floors to tiny live music venues, the city has a wide range of options for anyone looking for a great night out. Here are some of the most popular nightclubs and music venues in Bratislava:

Nightclubs:

The Club of Bratislava:
• Address: Rybné námestie 1, 811 01 Bratislava, Slovakia
• The Club is a well-known city nightclub with various dance floors playing a mix of electronic, dance, and pop music. With themed events and

frequent DJ performances, it creates a vibrant and dynamic environment.

Channels of Club Bratislava:
• Karadovova 4, Bratislava, Slovakia 821 08
Channels Club is a fashionable and appealing venue with modern décor and cutting-edge sound and lighting equipment. It has themed events, live performances, and DJ nights, all of which combine to create an unforgettable party atmosphere.

Subclub:
• Nábreie arm is the location. gen. L. Svobodu 811 02 Bratislava, Slovakia
• Subclub is a one-of-a-kind subterranean club in a former bomb bunker under Bratislava Castle. It is well-known for its wide range of music, which includes techno, drum & bass, and electronic music. Its unique charm is enhanced by its historic environment.

Musical Venues:

Ateliér, Babylon:
• Address: 14 Námestie SNP, Bratislava, Slovakia 811 01
• Ateliér Babylon is a multifunctional cultural centre that hosts live music concerts, theatrical

performances, and art exhibits. The theatre has a large stage and a lively atmosphere, making it a popular destination for both local and foreign performers.

The Majestic Music Club is a nightclub in New York City.
• Address: Karpatská 2, 811 05 Bratislava, Slovakia.
The Majestic music Club is a multipurpose facility that includes a large music hall as well as a smaller club area. It hosts concerts ranging from rock and pop to techno and indie music, drawing a wide range of music fans.

KC Dunaj:
• Address: 3 Nedbalova, Bratislava, Slovakia 811 01
In addition to being a nightclub, KC Dunaj is a cultural centre that hosts live music performances, film screenings, and art exhibits. It provides a platform for emerging local artists and bands, making it an excellent site for spotting fresh potential.

The Nu Spirit Lounge and Bar:
• Location: Medená 16, 811 02 Bratislava, Slovakia
• Description: In addition to being a well-known nightlife destination, Nu Spirit Bar & Lounge has live music performances and DJ sets that mix soul,

funk, jazz, and electronic music. Its nice and cosy atmosphere makes it a favourite among music lovers.

Please keep in mind that event and performance availability varies depending on the time of year and existing constraints. Examine the different venues' websites or social media pages for the most up-to-date schedule and information before planning your night out. Bratislava's nightlife provides something for everyone, whether you want to dance the night away at a nightclub or listen to live music in a small music venue.

Theatres and the Performing Arts

Bratislava has a vibrant cultural scene, with several theatres and performing arts institutions catering to a wide spectrum of creative impulses. The city has a range of options for theatre and performing arts enthusiasts, ranging from old theatres exhibiting classical performances to modern venues supporting contemporary performers. Here are some of the most significant theatres and performing arts venues in Bratislava:

Slovak National Theatre (Slovenské národné divadlo):
• Address: Pribinova 17, 811 09 Bratislava, Slovakia
• The Slovak National Theatre is the most important performing arts organisation in Slovakia. It is divided into three sections: theatre, opera, and ballet. The majestic neo-Renaissance building on the Danube River's banks houses a diverse mix of classical and modern art.

SND Nová budova (SND New Building):
• Address: Pribinova 17, 811 09 Bratislava, Slovakia
• The SND New Building is a contemporary construction located near the Slovak National Theatre. It provides extra performance space for modern theatre, experimental works, and cutting-edge cultural events.

Aréna Theatre (Divadlo Aréna):
• Viedenská cesta 10, 851 01 Bratislava, Slovakia
• Aréna Theatre is well-known for its experimental and cutting-edge theatrical works. It focuses on contentious plays and performances that challenge conventional theatrical standards and engage audiences in novel ways.

Astorka Korzo '90 Theatre (Divadlo Astorka Korzo '90):

- Address: 33 Námestie SNP, Bratislava, Slovakia 811 01
- Astorka Korzo '90 Theatre is a contemporary theatre that strives to produce socially relevant and aesthetic works. It features performances by Slovak and international playwrights addressing current issues and topics.

SND Ballet (Slovenského národného divadla):
- Address: Pribinova 17, 811 09 Bratislava, Slovakia
- Description: The Ballet ensemble of the Slovak National Theatre is made up of famous dancers and choreographers who work in both classical and modern dance works.

Elledanse • Divadlo Tanca (Elledanse • Dance Theatre):
- Mileticova 17/B, 821 08 Bratislava, Slovakia
- Elledanse is a non-profit theatre specialising in contemporary dance and physical theatre. It encourages innovation and experimentation by providing a platform for both established and emerging dance performers.

A4: Priestor pre sasn culture
- Address: Karpatská 2, 811 05 Bratislava, Slovakia.
- A4 is a multi-purpose cultural building that hosts a variety of performing arts events, including

theatre performances, concerts, dance performances, and multimedia works. It encourages experimental and alternative types of art.

By presenting a diverse range of creative expressions, Bratislava's theatres and performing arts venues contribute to the city's cultural vitality. Bratislava's stages always have something spectacular to offer, from classical classics to cutting-edge contemporary performances. Check the individual venues' websites or ticket offices for availability and information on upcoming events.

Chapter 11. Bratislava excursions

Vienna, Austria

Vienna, Austria, is conveniently located close to Bratislava and makes an excellent day excursion from the Slovakian capital. Tourists may immerse themselves in Vienna's imperial grandeur, cultural richness, and musical legacy in only a short trip. The following are some common day excursions from Bratislava to Vienna:

Vienna City Tour:
• Description: Visit the sights of Vienna on a guided city tour. The Schönbrunn Palace, St. Stephen's Cathedral, Hofburg Palace, and Vienna State Opera are all must-see attractions. Learn about the city's history, architecture, and musical traditions.

Vienna's Museums Quartier:
Spend the day in one of the world's biggest cultural complexes, the Museums Quartier. It is the location of many museums, galleries, and cultural organisations. Art enthusiasts can pay a visit to the Leopold Museum, MUMOK (Museum of Modern Art), and Kunsthalle Wien.

Opera or Concert in Vienna:
• Description: Experience the charm of Viennese music by attending a classical concert or opera performance. The Vienna State Opera and Musikverein are landmark theatres known for their excellent acoustics and world-class performances.

Seasonal Christmas Markets in Vienna:
• Description: Throughout the holiday season, Vienna's Christmas markets create a lively atmosphere. The Christkindlmarkt in front of City Hall and the market at Schönbrunn Palace are both quite popular, with beautiful decorations, crafts, and great refreshments available.

Schönbrunn Palace and Gardens:
• Description: Explore the sumptuous Schönbrunn Palace and its beautiful gardens, both of which are UNESCO World Heritage sites. Take a guided tour of the palace's magnificent apartments before strolling around the expansive grounds, which are ideal for a leisurely walk.

Wienerwald (Wienerwald):
• Description: Escape to the Vienna Woods, a peaceful wooded environment on the outskirts of Vienna. Hiking, nature walks, and breathtaking

views from the Kahlenberg and Leopoldsberg hills are all available.

The Danube River Cruise:
• Description: Bike from Bratislava to Vienna and enjoy amazing views along the Danube River. Explore Vienna's riverfront promenades and waterfront attractions.

Prater Amusement Park:
• Description: Spend a fun-filled day at the Prater, Vienna's famed amusement park. Take a ride on the renowned Wiener Riesenrad for spectacular city views.

Visit a Viennese Coffeehouse:
• Description: Experience the unique Viennese café culture at well-known establishments such as Café Central and Café Sacher. While enjoying delicious coffee and pastries, learn about the city's literary and cultural heritage.

Day journeys to Vienna from Bratislava take between one and two hours and may be taken by rail, bus, or car. Vienna, with its rich cultural history, gorgeous architecture, and pleasant surroundings, offers Bratislava visitors a fantastic day of exploration and discovery.

Budapest is Hungary's capital.

Budapest, Hungary's capital, is another interesting day trip from Bratislava. Budapest is famous for its beautiful architecture, hot spas, rich history, and vibrant culture. Visitors may enjoy the beauty and charm of this wonderful city, which is just a short distance from Bratislava. The following are some common day excursions from Bratislava to Budapest:

Walking Tour of Budapest:
• Description: Join a guided city tour of Budapest to see the city's most famous sites. The Buda Castle, Matthias Church, Hungarian Parliament Building, Heroes' Square, and Danube River embankments are all worth seeing. Explore the city's distinct history and eclectic architecture.

Hungarian Parliament Building:
• Description: Admire the splendour of the Hungarian Parliament, a neo-Gothic edifice beside the Danube River. Tour the magnificent interior, which includes the towering Dome Hall and the Hungarian Crown Jewels.

Széchenyi Thermal Bath:
- Description: Enjoy Budapest's famed thermal baths at Széchenyi Thermal Bath, one of Europe's biggest and most attractive thermal bath complexes. Relax in its hot pools for a one-of-a-kind wellness experience.

Buda Castle and Castle Hill:
- Tour Buda Castle, a beautiful castle complex with great city views. Explore Castle Hill, a UNESCO World Heritage site, and wander through gorgeous mediaeval roads lined with cafés, shops, and historical sites.

The Fisherman's Fortress:
- Description: Take in the fairytale-like architecture of Fisherman's Bastion, a terrace with neo-Gothic and neo-Romanesque characteristics. The Danube, the Hungarian Parliament, and the Pest side of the city can all be seen from here.

Sziget, Margaret (Margitsziget):
- Description: Unwind on Margaret Island, a recreation haven in the midst of the Danube River. The greenery, walking paths, gardens, and ancient ruins make it a perfect location for relaxation and leisure activities.

Danube River Cruise:
• Description: Take a picturesque Danube River cruise from Bratislava to Budapest. Throughout the ride, take in breathtaking views of the countryside and the riverside splendor. When you arrive, explore Budapest's riverfront and promenades.

Hsök tere (The Square of Heroes):
• Heroes' Square is a large square featuring sculptures of Hungarian historical figures. It is a well-known landmark in Budapest and a symbol of Hungary's national history.

Day trips to Budapest from Bratislava may be taken by rail, bus, or car, and the travel takes around two to three hours. Because of its rich history, gorgeous architecture, thermal spas, and bustling atmosphere, Budapest is an excellent choice for a day of exploration and cultural immersion.

Bratislava's Surrounding Castles

Bratislava is surrounded by magnificent castles and historical sites, making it an ideal starting point for exploring Slovakia's rich cultural history. A day excursion from Bratislava to these castles enables visitors to journey back in time and immerse themselves in the country's distinctive heritage. Here are a some of the magnificent castles that may be visited as day excursions from Bratislava:

Devin Castle (Hrad Devin):
• Description: Devin Castle is a landmark of Slovakia's historic history, located just outside of Bratislava. The castle, perched on a ledge above the confluence of the Danube and Morava rivers, has commanding views of the surrounding countryside. Visitors may explore the relics, climb the towers, and learn about the history of the area.

Bratislava Castle (Bratislavsky hrad):
• Description: Bratislava Castle is located on a hill overlooking the city of Bratislava. The castle is notable for its dazzling white walls and four corner towers. The castle reveals details about Slovakia's royal past, and the panoramic views of Bratislava from the castle hill are breathtaking.

Erven Kame Castle:
• Erven Kame Castle, located about 40 km northeast of Bratislava, is a one-of-a-kind stronghold with a history dating back to the 13th century. The interiors of the castle, particularly the Knight's Hall and the Baroque chapel, have been meticulously preserved. The magnificence of the

castle is enhanced by the nearby vineyards and wonderful views.

Smolenice Castle (Smolenick zámok):
• Smolenice Castle, 60 km northeast of Bratislava, is a lovely Romantic-style castle surrounded by a garden. It offers a peaceful vacation in nature as well as an insight into the lifestyle of the Slovak elite. The castle's spires and turrets give it a fantasy feel.

Bojnick zámok (Bojnick zámok): a zámok (a zámok) is a kind
• Description: Bojnice Castle is one of Slovakia's most visited castles, located around 150 km northeast of Bratislava. It is usually regarded as a fairytale castle due to its distinctive design and exquisite grounds. The castle houses the Slovak National Museum's Museum of Bojnice, which houses historical and artistic treasures.

Beckov (Beckovsk) hrad:
Beckov Castle is located on a limestone cliff above the settlement of Beckov, some 100 km northwest of Bratislava. The castle's strategic location provides stunning views of the surrounding countryside. It is an excellent site for both history buffs and environment lovers.

Nitra Castle (Nitriansky hrad):
• Description: Nitra Castle is one of Slovakia's oldest castles, located around 100 km east of Bratislava. It has historical exhibits as well as a vantage point with views over Nitra and the Nitra River valley.

These castles are a beautiful and interesting day excursion from Bratislava, and they give insight into Slovakia's past. Whether you like history, architecture, or just seeing beautiful landscapes, a visit to these castles will leave you with lasting memories of your stay in Slovakia.

Chapter 12. Helpful Information

Emergency Contact Information

It is essential to have access to emergency contacts while visiting a new region in case of any unanticipated incidents. You should be aware of the following emergency contacts while visiting Bratislava:

Services such as police, fire, and ambulance:
• Emergency: 112 (Use this number in an emergency to connect to the appropriate agencies).

Bratislava police:
• Phone: +421 2 5441 0000

Medical Emergencies and Ambulances:
• In case of an emergency, dial 112
• Emergency Medical Service (Záchranná zdravotná sluba • ZZS): 155

Fire Department (Hasisk zbor):
• In case of an emergency, dial 112
• 150 for fire and rescue emergencies

Consulates and Embassies from other countries:
• If you want help while traveling, have the contact information for your country's embassy or consulate in Slovakia handy.
• Contact information for your country's embassy or consulate in Bratislava may be found on your country's official government website.

Visitors Should Know:
• Bratislava Tourist Board:
• Phone: +421 2 161 186
• Contact us at info@visitbratislava.com.

Poison Control Unit:
• Phone: +421 2 4925 1122

Roadside Assistance:
• Assistance: 112
• For non-emergency road assistance, contact vehicle clubs such as the Slovak Car Club (Slovenski Autoklub • Záchranná Sluba) at +421 2 521 11111.

Keep a written copy of critical emergency contacts on hand, as well as their phone numbers, in case your phone's battery dies or you experience connectivity problems. Consider alerting a trusted friend or family member about your holiday plans and supplying them with your itinerary and contact information, particularly if you plan to visit exotic locations or engage in outdoor activities. Having emergency contacts on hand may provide you piece of mind when traveling to Bratislava.

Health and safety advice

Any trip must include considerations for one's health and safety. When visiting Bratislava or on any other vacation, it is essential to prioritise your health. Here are some health and safety tips:

Before you depart, make sure you have enough travel insurance that covers medical emergencies, trip cancellations, and other unexpected tragedies.

Vaccinations & Health Precautions: Consult your doctor or a travel clinic about any required immunisations or health precautions for Slovakia.

Bring critical medical information, such as allergies, medications, and emergency contacts, in case of a medical emergency.

Save important emergency contacts, such as local emergency services (112), your country's embassy or consulate, and your hotel's contact information.

Water Safety: While tap water in Bratislava is generally safe to drink, bottled water is recommended if you are unsure.

Personal Safety: Although Bratislava is a secure city, employ common sense by avoiding poorly lit places at night and keeping an eye on your possessions in congested areas.

Currency and valuables: Use ATMs in well-lit, secure areas and avoid exhibiting large amounts of cash or valuables in public.

Cross streets with caution, use marked pedestrian crossings and keep an eye out for automobiles, particularly if using public transit.

Sun Protection: During the summer months, use sunscreen, wear hats, and stay hydrated to protect yourself from the sun's rays.

Food Safety: Be cautious with street food while enjoying the local cuisine. Select eateries that follow adequate sanitary practises, and avoid eating raw or undercooked food.

Language: Learn a few basic Slovak terms or have a translation tool on available to help with discussions.

Respect Local Customs: When visiting religious sites, keep local customs, traditions, and attire norms in mind.

Use reputable cab services, and if you must use public transit, be aware of your surroundings and keep your belongings safe.

Weather Precautions: Dress appropriately for the weather and be ready for unexpected changes.

You can ensure a safe and enjoyable vacation to Bratislava by being educated, taking necessary precautions, and always alert of your surroundings. Remember that safety is a shared responsibility, and being proactive may help you make the most of your vacation.

Etiquette and local customs

Understanding local etiquette and traditions is essential for displaying respect for the culture and people of Bratislava. Here are some important etiquette guidelines and conventions to follow during your visit:

Handshakes are the most common kind of greeting when meeting someone. Maintain eye contact and speak in a kind tone.

Slovaks are formal in their relationships, particularly when meeting someone for the first time or while dealing with a financial situation. Unless instructed otherwise, address someone by their title and surname.

In Slovakia, punctuality is essential for appointments, meetings, and social events. It shows concern for other people's time and duties.

Dining Etiquette: Wait for the host to invite you to the table before taking your seat. Table manners may be stiff at times, so avoid resting your elbows on the table and eat with your hands visible.

Tipping is customarily expected at restaurants, cafés, and pubs. The standard tip is 10% of the whole bill. Some restaurants may charge a service fee, so check your statement carefully before tipping.

Learn a few simple words in Slovak, the official language, as a sign of respect. The indigenous will appreciate your efforts to communicate in their language.

Slovaks like to dress correctly and modestly, particularly in formal settings. When visiting churches or religious places, dress appropriately and check for any special dress requirements.

Respect for Religion: Because Slovakia is mostly Catholic, tourists should be courteous of churches and religious places. Dress modestly to avoid loud talks and unpleasant behaviours.

Maintain an appropriate level of loudness in public places such as subways and museums. Avoid noisy or loud behaviour that may annoy others.

When welcomed to someone's house, it is customary to offer a little present for the host, such as flowers, chocolates, or a bottle of wine.

Indoors, it is customary to remove your shoes before entering some areas, such as private homes or religious institutions.

Personal Space: Be respectful of others' personal space and avoid approaching them too closely, particularly if you don't know them well.

Queuing: Slovaks value orderly queuing. Wait patiently in lines in shops, public transportation, and other places where queuing is required.

Always get permission before shooting people, particularly in close-up images. Be mindful of any photography restrictions at certain locations or institutions.

By following these local traditions and etiquette, you will show respect for the local culture and people, and you will most likely have a more enjoyable and rewarding experience in Bratislava. Keep in mind that cultural understanding is essential for making genuine connections with people and learning about the city's way of life.

Effective Expressions

Learning a few key words in the local language will improve your vacation experience and allow you to interact with the people of Bratislava. Here are some key Slovak phrases to know before your trip:

Greetings - Ahoj (ah-hoy)
Dobré ráno (DOH-breh RAH-noh) - Good morning.
Dobr de (DOH-bree dehn) means "good day."
Dobr veer (DOH-bree VEH-chehr) - good evening
Dovidenia (doh-VEE-deh-nyah) says goodbye.
Please - Prosm (pronounced PROH-seem)
Thank you very much - akujem (JAH-koo-yehm).
Yes/no (AH-noh)
New Year's Eve (NYE)
Please excuse me - Prepáte (PREH-paach-teh).
I apologise - utujem (LOO-too-yem).
Do you understand English? - Do you speak English? (AHN-glit-skee AHN-voh-ree-teh poh AHN-glit-skee?)

I'm not sure - Nerozumiem (neh-roh-ZOO-myem)
How much does this cost? - Koko na stoj? (KOH-ly-koh STOH-yee?)
Where can I find a loo? - Where is the toaleta? (Can you say TOH-ah-leh-tah?)

Can you help me? - Could you please assist me? (MOH-zheh-teh poh-MOH-tst?
I need the services of a doctor - Potrebujem lekára (poht-REH-boo-yem LEH-ka-rah).
Help! - Pomoc! (POH-mots!)
Cheers! - Thank you! (Na zdrah-vee!)

Bratislava is my favourite city - bim Bratislavu (LOO-beem Brah-tis-lah-voo).

These important words will be useful during your visit to Bratislava. Even if you don't understand Slovak, the locals will appreciate your attempts to communicate in their language. As with any language, a smile and a friendly demeanour go a long way towards creating lasting relationships with the people you encounter on your travels.

Chapter 13. Cambus for FUTO join cages for a Memorable Vacation

Hidden Gems and Off-the-Beaten-Path Locations.

Exploring Bratislava's hidden treasures and off-the-beaten-path locations may result in one-of-a-kind and unforgettable experiences. Here are a few lesser-known places to visit:

The Blue Church (Modr kostolik):
This remarkable Art Nouveau church, properly known as St. Elizabeth's Church, stands out with its stunning blue exterior and exquisite ornamentation. It's a little out of the way from the city centre, which makes it a hidden treasure for architectural enthusiasts and photographers.

Slavin Memorial:
While not completely hidden, the Slavin Memorial provides a peaceful respite from the hustle and bustle of the city. This WWII monument and military cemetery provides an excellent view of Bratislava as well as a tranquil setting for reflection.

Janka Kráa (Janko Krá Park) is unhappy:
The oldest public park in Central Europe, this lovely park near the Danube River. It's ideal for a leisurely walk, a peaceful picnic, or just taking in the river views.

Sandberg:
The Sandberg is a man-made hill formed from WWII bombing wreckage. It offers a panoramic view over Bratislava and is a great place to get away from the city for nature enthusiasts and hikers.

The SNP Bridge Observation Deck:
Take a lift to the top of the iconic SNP Bridge (UFO Bridge) for a panoramic view of the city. The observation deck offers a unique view of Bratislava's skyline and the Danube River.

Kozia Brána (The Goat's Gate):
This hidden treasure is a little tunnel in Old Town with a goat stone sculpture. It's easy to overlook, yet locating it might be a fantastic treasure hunt.

Capuchin Church and Monastery:
This secluded church and monastery complex, located away from the major tourist attractions,

offers a peaceful haven as well as the chance to see stunning artwork and Baroque architecture.

Chatam Sofer Memorial:
This lovely and historic Jewish cemetery is dedicated to the famous rabbi Chatam Sofer. It's a hidden gem in Bratislava where you may learn about Jewish history.

Medická Záhrada (Medical Garden):
This beautiful park in the city centre is a favorite place for folks to relax and enjoy nature. It's a lovely spot for a leisurely stroll or a tranquil time away from the rush and bustle.

The Kamzik Television Tower:
Take a short trek to Kamzk Hill to see the TV Tower. In addition to stunning views, the area has walking trails and a café serving traditional Slovak cuisine.

Exploring these hidden jewels will give you a better understanding of Bratislava's rich history, beautiful surroundings, and local culture. Don't be afraid to go beyond the tourist traps to discover the city's lesser-known gems.

Photographic Tips

Photography is an excellent way to capture the beauty of Bratislava and enjoy your vacation memories. Here are some tips to help you take stunning photos on your trip:

Golden Hour: During the "golden hour," which occurs between dawn and twilight, take advantage of the tranquil, pleasant light. This lighting adds a beautiful sheen and enhances the colours in your photographs.

Rule of Thirds: When arranging your photographs, follow the rule of thirds. Consider dividing the space into nine equal halves and placing your topic or areas of interest along or at the intersections of the grid lines.

To frame your topic, you might use natural elements, buildings, or other artefacts. Framing your images adds depth and draws attention to the main focal point.

Capture the details: Don't forget to photograph the minute details that identify Bratislava. Take note of architectural features, street art, local food, and everyday scenes.

Leading lines, such as highways, fences, or riverbanks, may be used to draw the viewer's attention into the picture and create the illusion of depth and movement.

Experiment with Angles: To add variation to your images, shoot from various angles and perspectives. Get down, photograph from above, or experiment with tilting your camera for novel effects.

Use a Tripod: In low-light situations or for shooting lengthy exposures, use a tripod to keep your camera stable and eliminate blur.

Include people: Including people in your images may give them a sense of size and narrative. Capture real moments of locals or travel companions to bring your images to life.

Avoid Overediting: While post-processing may improve your photos, be wary of overediting. Keep a realistic picture of the city while preserving the inherent beauty of the places you shoot.

Respect Local Culture: Always get permission before photographing anyone, particularly locals.

Be mindful of cultural customs and personal privacy.

Wait for the perfect time to take the perfect image. Patience may pay off in the form of more clear and fascinating visuals.

Explore Different Neighbourhoods: Venture beyond the famous tourist attractions to discover hidden corners and less-photographed regions that provide a fresh perspective on Bratislava.

The most important thing to remember is to have fun while capturing the soul of Bratislava via your lens. Experiment with different approaches, embrace spontaneity, and allow your imagination run wild to create a collection of one-of-a-kind images from your travels.

Final Thoughts on Bratislava

As the sun set below the horizon, casting a warm golden glow over Bratislava, I stood on the Danube's banks, taking in the city's stunning surroundings. My journey through this little town had been nothing short of remarkable, full with hidden jewels and unforgettable events.

I was transported back in time as I strolled through the Old Town's cobblestone passageways, surrounded by the beautiful façades of centuries-old buildings. As each step revealed a new narrative inscribed on the walls, I could almost hear the whispers of the city's rich past. I gasped at the fairytale-like splendour of the Blue Church, feeling as if I had walked into an artist's masterpiece. As I toured the busy markets and colourful squares, the friendly people shared their stories with warmth and pride, making me feel like a member of their community. The perfume of freshly brewed coffee and the sound of laughing from busy cafés filled the air, inviting me to experience the spirit of Slovakian hospitality.

Off the beaten road, I discovered stunning perspectives like the serene Sandberg and the Slavin Memorial, where I felt tranquilly and a deep feeling of history. Hiking up Kamzk Hill, I stood atop the TV Tower, recording the cityscape from above, and felt grateful for the opportunity to observe Bratislava's splendor from such heights.

The Danube River ran freely, providing a vital link between the city's history and future. I walked over the world-famous SNP Bridge to the UFO observation deck, where the city stretched out beneath me like a living tapestry. As darkness struck, I found myself in the tranquil courtyard of the Capuchin Church, bathed in the soft glow of candles. The church's melancholic beauty welcomed me, giving me moments of reflection and gratitude for the journey I'd taken.

Bratislava had braided its way into my heart, leaving an unforgettable mark on my soul, with its genuineness and hidden secrets. With its historic castles, twisting alleyways, and warm-hearted residents, this city had not only awakened my eyes to its beauty, but also instilled my soul with memories that would last a lifetime. As I wished Bratislava goodnight, I knew I'd carry its charm, legends, and the spirit of my personalized experience with me wherever my travels took me next.

Printed in Great Britain
by Amazon